Stock Charting Book for Beginners

A great source for learning charting analysis for successful stock trades. (Candlesticks, Bollinger Bands, Keltner Channel The Squeeze, Scanning, and more)

Kakkle Publications

Legal Notice:

Disclaimer Notice:

Published in the United States of America

ISBN: 979-8-9859579-5-2

Contents

Stock Charting Book for Beginners

A great source for learning charting analysis for successful stock trades. (Candlesticks, Bollinger Bands, Keltner Channel The Squeeze, Scanning, and more)

By Kakkle Publications

Introduction

"*In trading, you have to be defensive and aggressive at the same time. If you are not aggressive, you are not going to make money, and if you are not defensive, you are not going to keep the money.*"

-Ray Dalio.

If you've spent any time in the trading *or* investment world, you've probably heard the phrase, "Never trade with money you can't afford to lose. " Because of the inherent danger in the type of investment you intend to make, this is a popular phrase and cautious words to heed. You may have also heard about traders losing all of their money, but the truth is that you are most likely not being given the complete picture.

Many people make a living and do extremely well by trading stocks. They have spent time studying the market and developing winning tactics that have provided them with excellent results. Do these people have losses? Of course they do, but their key to success is that the gains they make vastly outnumber those losses.

You might be asking how they manage to accomplish it with all the risks involved. They have learned to respect the market and the risks that come with trading. You're reading this book because you want to be a successful stock trader but **may not be sure** which approach you should use.

You've become interested in technical analysis and chart patterns and you'd like to learn more, particularly about how to use them to make more profitable deals. Let me just add that you are already on the right track. However, for the few who are still unconvinced, there are three basic categories of security market analysis: fundamental, quantitative, and technical analysis.

Fundamental Analysis

Fundamental analysis focuses on the elements that will affect a company's stock price in the future. Management method, financial statements, earnings, goods, and industry are only a few examples. To determine if a company's inherent value is overvalued or under-priced, a study of its intrinsic value is performed.

Decisions and plans are based on analyzed statistics and publicly available information about the organization. Unlike technical analysis, which is based on historical data, fundamental analysis is based on both historical and current data, and it is more useful for long-term investments.

Quantitative Analysis

Quantitative analysis focuses on using mathematics and statistics to assess the price or value of financial assets such as stocks, options, and other financial assets. Quantitative analysis, sometimes known as "quants," creates algorithms and computational methods using a variety of information, including historical investment and stock market data. Investors can use the data generated by these computer models to examine investment and trading opportunities such as entry, exit, take profit, and stop-loss signals. The basic goal of quantitative analysis is to produce lucrative trading signals for traders using accessible information and metrics.

Technical Analysis

Chart patterns, candlestick patterns, demand and supply, volume, support and resistance, and other indicators are all studied using technical analysis. Although properly predicting the market is difficult, technical analysis can help make the work easier and more accurate in some cases.

Technical analysis gives you an understanding of the human emotions that influence trading and how it is rooted in psychology. Technical analysis uses historical data to forecast a stock's future price, removing the necessity for fundamental study.

Stock, Equity, Commodity, and Options traders mainly use technical analysis to predict short and long-term price actions. More traders are turning to technical analysis to help them execute more profitable trades. As a result, there has been a surge in interest in mastering technical analysis and chart patterns.

Trading the market is complex, and only the most serious investors should be doing it. With the proper examination of historical data, you can predict price behavior and enter more winning trades.

In this book, we'll discuss technical indicators and how they may help you discover price fluctuations, breakouts, trends, range, and momentum, among other things. Some of the reasons why traders and investors prefer technical analysis to other trading tactics are listed below.

Psychology

Technical analysis and chart patterns help you gain a better grasp of investor and trader behavior in relation to a specific market You learn about what they've done in the past and what they're likely to do in the future.

Trend Analysis

Trend Analysis is one of the most important advantages of technical analysis and chart patterns. You can predict future price action using chart patterns, which provides you with an advantage as a trader or investor and positions you for significant profits. This book will teach you how to recognize the three sorts of trends that occur over the life of a stock.

Entry and Exit Points

Knowing when to enter a trade and when to exit one, whether in a lucrative or losing position, can mean the difference between succeeding in trading or losing a lot of money. This book will show you numerous instances of how to determine the proper entry and exit strategies.

You'll learn how to use chart patterns effectively to spot traps and false signals and to pinpoint these periods. We will show you how to spot breakouts, ranges, momentum, and trends using technical indicators. You'll also discover how to trade in a market that appears to be ambiguous.

Early Signals

Another advantage of chart patterns and technical analysis is the ability to detect and anticipate a trend reversal before it occurs. As a trader, this is one of the most exciting times in the market since you have the opportunity to profit significantly.

This book will teach you how to recognize these signs and make the most of them. We will also demonstrate how to use Price-Volume

Analysis to determine when the market is about to make a huge move and when a trend is tiring and losing steam.

Money Management

You can rapidly select how long you want to stay in a trade using technical analysis, allowing you to avoid future losses. Knowing when to leave a losing deal has become more crucial to a trader than making profits in the market. These are only a few of the topics covered in this book. You'll know how to manage risk.

Informative

Traders and investors can use chart patterns and technical analysis to get more information to assist them to make better decisions. Chart patterns and the information they provide can benefit all sorts of traders, including swing, intraday, short, and long-term traders.

Technical charts provide precise information that can help you make the best decision and improve your portfolio. Several areas on the chart, such as the support and resistance levels, contain a wealth of information that can help you make better selections. This book will teach you everything you need to know. We will show you how to make informed judgments by studying candlestick patterns, volatility, volume, and other indicators.

The more you practice, the better you will get and the more misconceptions about chart patterns will be dispelled. Below are some of the myths of technical analysis.

Technical Analysis is Best for Intraday Trading

This is the most typical error used by those who do not have a thorough understanding of how technical analysis works. Technical analysis can be used by all sorts of traders, from short-term to long-term traders, in their strategies. Technical analysis existed long before the computer was built, and it has long been used by many successful investors and traders. We will show you various examples of long-term investments and transactions.

Only Retail Traders Use Technical Analysis.

Retail traders, without a doubt, utilize technical analysis to design their trade tactics, but hedge funds and investment banks also use it extensively. These big spenders have a dedicated staff of experts who design trading strategies and enter profitable trades for their company and investors using chart patterns and technical tools.

The Low Success Rate Myth

This is another myth perpetuated by skeptics of technical analysis, but the truth is that technical analysis and chart patterns have helped a lot of traders make an abundance of money. Technical analysis was used by some of the most successful individuals and institutional traders to build their fortunes.

Technical Analysis Provides Easy Money

This is a common internet falsehood propagated by people advertising technical analysis courses and training, but they have never done a dollar transaction in a real market. To succeed in the market, we will demonstrate that technical analysis necessitates extensive training, deep understanding, complete information, and good money management abilities. You'll notice that we highlight the importance of doing a proper demo trading for at least three months and maybe six months before investing real money.

Technical Analysis Provides Accurate Signals

This is just another misunderstanding that has resulted in millions of dollars in losses and is promoted by people who have not invested a single dime in the market. Only inexperienced traders can accurately predict a price action or signal. If necessary, the most experienced traders will specify a range, which they will back up with a disclaimer.

There are no instruments or robots that can produce a clear signal; you may come across something that can provide entry and exit signals for a limited period of time

, but they are never sustainable. To be a good trader, you must be willing to put in the effort.

What You Will Get from this Book

In addition to everything mentioned above, here are some key take-aways you will get from this book.

- You will become familiar with all the technical vocabulary used in technical analysis, including chart patterns, candle-sticks, and more. Some of these names may have perplexed you in the past, but they've been streamlined for your convenience.

- You'll learn about candlestick patterns, their history, and why they're one of the most significant stock-chart tools. Every candlestick has various meanings, which you will discover in this book.

- What are chart patterns, and why are they important to your stock trading success? This book will teach you that, as well as provide several examples. You will be able to recognize and analyze chart patterns after reading this book.

- The distinction between stop order limits and limit orders is frequently misunderstood by newcomers to the stock market. In a separate chapter of this book, we spend considerable time describing the difference.

- You'll also learn how to spot a bullish or bearish market, as well as how to measure the volume of activities and actions that lead to a range and, eventually, a breakout.

- You will also learn how to identify and take advantage of overbought and oversold price levels in the market.

- Simple Moving Averages and Exponential Averages will be covered. We spend considerable time discussing how to set them up, how to calculate them, and when to utilize them.

- We discuss some of the best technical indicators available and how you can combine them for the best result.

- You'll learn a lot about the Keltner Channels' unique features and how to make the most of them. We also discussed how to use the Bollinger Bands in conjunction with the Keltner Channel to achieve excellent results.

About The Author

Kakkle is a leading publishing firm comprised of successful investors and traders with extensive financial and investment knowledge. They are passionate about developing finance books that allow people to start making money using the principles they learn.

These authors are seasoned investors and traders with years of trading expertise; they've spent their time deciphering the difficulties that keep people from profiting from stock trading. They are dedicated to assisting individuals, both young and old, in comprehending the dynamics of wealth generation and financial independence.

You will sense the author's enthusiasm and dedication to wealth building and management as you turn the pages. As a stock market authority, they want to set your mind at ease and comfort you that if they can do it, so can you.

You've chosen the right book! It's now or never to achieve financial independence.

Chapter One

Chapter 1

Breaking Down the Lingo

Introduction to Stock Charts

Charts are useful because they make it easier for us to visualize and arrange stock prices. Technical analysis would be nearly impossible to comprehend without charts because you'd be left with a vast, complex, and dull theoretical explanation of rates that was disorganized.

Charts are the most common technical analysis tool; they help you visualize price movements by presenting past historical market data for the underlying financial instrument on a graph. This pictorial representation makes it easier to distinguish between rare and common price patterns. Technical analysis focuses on identifying trends, momentum, support, and resistance on a price chart in order to enter and exit more lucrative trades. The chart can be compared to a jigsaw board game in which if you can fit the pieces together correctly, the picture turns out beautifully and you feel good about yourself.

In addition, charts can be used to answer questions such as, *Where is the stock going? What is the current state of the market?* The answer to these and other issues is ultimately determined by time, and charts can help you better grasp time. Traders can easily create a price history and forecast using charts, allowing them to make better and more educated transactions.

Why is the Chart Important?

If you've ever heard the phrase "what goes around comes around," you know what we are talking about. It's accurate and can be used to create chart patterns. Because history tends to repeat itself, the chart makes it easier to anticipate when the "turning around" will occur. Charts are like maps, and we see these patterns in the financial markets time after time. Price movements follow predictable patterns, and charts are the greatest method to visualize this recurrence.

An individual's viewpoint or experience is used to interpret charts and applications. The beauty of a chart pattern is that it will finally play out whether your interpretation was true or not. If you had hesitated previously, it may not be too late to make a lucrative option. What makes the difference is being able to predict and profit from a market move before it occurs.

Below are some other factors of the chart.

- Stock chart records price history and volume to help you determine if the stock is appreciating or depreciating.

- More information on the price volume can help you know if the stock is acting normally or abnormally.

- If the stock or organization is falling in or out of favor with investors.

- You can also determine the start and ending prices ahead.

Predictive and Foreshadowing Elements

Imagine being able to predict the future. Consider how much money you could make if you could predict or have advance knowledge of upcoming stock market happenings. That's what the chart allows you to do. The chart is used for a variety of purposes by stock traders, but the end goal remains the same.

The stock charts allow traders to see what is going on in order to make educated guesses about the future of a stock price. Stock charts are the major source of data for most Day Traders when constructing their approach. A Day Trader will examine the stock pattern, assess the volume, and take note of price zones that are relevant. This can help you increase your chances of making more money before you enter a trade.

How to Read a Chart

Regardless of whether you are a novice or an expert, the fundamentals of chart reading always include the concepts of trend, support, and resistance. If you can grasp the concepts of these three areas, you will be well on your way to becoming a successful stock trader. Observing the price of a particular stock's highs and lows over a sustained period might help you identify an upward or downward trend in the stock. When a stock's highs and lows rise in tandem, it's an indication of a rising price trend, also known as an uptrend, in the stock market. In contrast, it demonstrates a downtrend or a net price decline when it makes lower highs and lower lows, indicating a price loss.

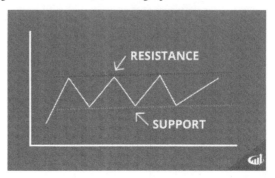

Price Support Levels

When the price of a stock appears to consistently bounce about a certain price range, that price range may be the support level. The support level is the price at which more buyers or investors are willing to purchase further shares of a company. It's a sign of an uptrend when a support level continues to advance higher. It suggests that buyers are growing impatient and upping their bids to buy at greater prices, attracting additional liquidity.

However, if the stock does not close at higher prices, then a pivotal reaction will develop, and the resistance level with either breakout and climb to higher prices (also known as an ascending triangle pattern), or the resistance will be too powerful and the price declines.

Price Resistance Levels

A resistance in action is when the stock price consistently falls inside a certain price range or finds it difficult to rise above that level. Buyers attempting to sell their long positions or boost their short positions are at a resistance level. A downtrend is defined as a price that continually declines downward. It indicates that sellers are becoming irritated and are willing to sell their positions for a lower price.

Breakout and Breakdowns

As previously stated, price levels of support and resistance are price levels that consistently reject attempts to climb above (resistance) or fall below (support). In other words, support is the price level below which the stock price cannot fall, and resistance is the price level above which the stock price cannot climb. To be clear, support is on the decline, while opposition is on the rise. The longer these price levels remain stable, the greater the likelihood of a subsequent breakout or breakdown.

It's similar to driving and attempting to get away from something; when you come across a barrier, you have to choose between driving through the barrier or turning around. If you choose to drive through, it indicates that you wish to break free; ideally, your vehicle is capable of doing so.

Breakout occurs when price levels of resistance are no longer able to hold; this indicates that buyers are getting more decisive and jumping off the fence, while short sellers are purchasing to cover their positions in the market. A breakdown, on the other hand, occurs when the support price levels are no longer able to hold. Panic selling occurs as more sellers dump their shares, while short sellers increase the size of their position, which leads to an even greater increase in volume.

Divergence patterns employing indicators in comparison to prices use trend lines to represent the indicator peaks and bottoms in order to illustrate indicator support or resistance on the chart. Whenever a specific price level is breached, the price charts have a reaction as a result of this. These are only temporary support and resistance levels since indicators shift frequently due to the fact that time is a dynamic component. The MACD is frequently utilized for divergence indications, which are created by comparing the oscillator peaks and valleys to the price activity.

Trends

Investopedia defines a trend as *"the overall direction of a market or an asset's price. In technical analysis, trends are identified by trendlines or price action that highlight when the price is making higher swing highs and higher swing lows for an uptrend, or lower swing lows and lower swing highs for a downtrend."*

Trend Lines

Tradelines are frequently used by traders to assess their trades in order to better grasp the trend or to catch a trend early, as we say in the market, trading range, support, and resistance levels on a chart. Trend line features are available on most trading platforms, and some trading platforms even offer tools that can assist you in drawing trend lines manually. As a result of subjective start points, automatic trend lines may not always be accurate. Trend lines are drawn manually by experienced traders for the sake of precision and speed.

How to Draw Trend Lines

Trend lines can be drawn in two directions: diagonally and horizontally. A basic trend line connects the lowest lows on candlestick or bar charts from left to right and can also be used to connect highs. It's worth noting that not every candle falls within the trend line. The idea is to join the body's lowest and highest points, or wicks. This will result in the creation of a trading range or a trade channel. The higher the trend line, the more resistance there is, and the lower the trend line, the more support there is. Multiple trend lines with different starting points are possible, but you must be careful not to create too many lines.

Trend Line Starting Points

Any trend line's starting point is determined by the trader's experience and trading pattern. If a trend line is drawn too far back in time, it can result in ambiguous channels. The highs and lows of a certain time frame are usually a good place to start. You can have different time frames as the range gets closer or the intervals get smaller. You may identify if a potential chart pattern is forming or has formed using a trend line.

Diagonal Trend Lines

The most difficult part of drawing a trend is deciding where to begin the plot point. Working from the left to the right of your chart is a good rule of thumb. That implies you'll start with either the high or low of a range that starts on the left side and connects the significant lows in a single diagonal line. If the stock is trending downward, for example, you should link the highs to reflect the lower highs.

Practical Example

In the chart below, you can see a clear example of a trend line in a downtrend and an uptrend

This is a basic trend line and some of the easiest to draw:

1. You can see three swing highs on the downtrend

2. You can see three swing lows on the uptrend

Please take note of the following;

- Trend lines in a **downward** trend are drawn **above the price.**

- Trend lines in an **upward trend** are drawn **below the price.**

The trend line is determined by the highs on a falling trend and the lows on a rising trend. However, depending on the trend's direction, you should utilize three highs and three lows to make your trend line credible. The more times the prices cross the trend lines, the more likely it is that they are being used as support and resistance by traders.

Uptrends

An uptrend is made up of higher highs and higher lows. You can reflect this by drawing a diagonal trend line linking the lows from the left of your chart to the right. See the chart below

For the most effective results, ensure to have three points of contact with the trend line. You can measure or confirm the effectiveness by the magnitude of the break. Sometimes, when a significant price movement occurs and breaks the trend line, it's proof that it was drawn correctly.

Downtrends

Downtrends are made up of lower highs and lower lows. You can show this by drawing a trend line from left to right. A downward trend remains intact until the upper trend line resistance is breached, at which point you can be on the lookout for a trend reversal.

Horizontal Trend Line

If a stock price is trading below a horizontal trend line, it can act as solid resistance, and if prices are trading above it, it can act as powerful support. These lines are useful in ascending and descending triangle patterns where the resistance remains constant but the pullbacks become shallower until the horizontal trend line is breached, indicating a trend reversal.

Upper and Lower Trendlines

Is it required to show upper and lower trend lines on every chart? Remember that the goal of a trend line is to record similar price periods in order to confirm a trend, whether it applies solely to support or only to resistance. A single trend line is frequently sufficient. You'll come across situations where all you need is one support or resistance line. In fact, if one side is stable and the other is unstable, having multiple trend lines may do more harm than good to your trades. When likely patterns such as triangles, flags, or wedges are emerging, only utilize two trendlines.

Stock Trends Across Multiple Time Frames

A stock might be in both a downward and upward trend at the same time. Confusing? Let's get to the bottom of it.

Trading charts come in a variety of time ranges, ranging from 1 minute to monthly. So it's a matter of prioritizing the time span you want to focus on. That is also dependent on the trade technique you intend to use. Long-term investors target longer time horizons for their strategy, such as weekly and monthly time frames. Intra-day traders prefer intra-day time frames, which range from 1-minute to 60-minute charts, whereas swing traders prefer daily and hourly time frames.

As a result, a downtrend that appears on an intra-day chart may appear to be an uptrend when examined on a longer time frame chart.

Technical Analysis

The term appears difficult and uninspired, but once you get past the complication, it's easy to understand. Technical analysis is a trading approach that examines statistical trends from trading activity such as volume and price movement to appraise and discover trading opportunities. Technical analysis simply means that a stock's prior price activity and price are useful indicators that can be utilized to forecast the stock's future price behavior.

To get the most out of technical analysis, you'll need a chart and some statistical indicators to figure out where price support, resistance, range, and trend are. The analysis focuses solely on the company's pricing activities and has nothing to do with who the CEO is or how many employees they have across the country. The emphasis is on the historical significance of price patterns and behaviors in forecasting the stock's possible direction so that the trader may profit and make effective entry and exit decisions.

How Does Technical Analysis Work?

Dinosaurs can't walk through the sand without leaving a trace. Institutions, mutual and hedge funds, and the key movers and shakers of stock values are all mentioned in this context. Technical analysis is a method of interpreting or speculating on the supply and demand forces that drive stock values.

In essence, technical analysis is the process of using charts and indicators to visually track the dinosaurs' footprints and actions in order to find price areas of high interest for buying and selling. History repeats itself when it comes to stocks and other financial instruments.

Who are the Users of Technical Analysis?

Technical analysis is not for everyone, but if you trade or invest in the stock market or other tradable financial instruments, you should learn about it, even if only at the fundamental levels. Assume your fund is invested in a position that is subject to price fluctuation. In this instance, technical analysis can assist you in making informed judgments about how much to risk and what to expect from a certain transaction.

Stocks represent a company's basic business and operations, but its stock price reflects the firm's insight and future valuation as well as its success. Between the two, there is always a discrepancy. Technical analysis also aids in determining the source of the gap and the number of opportunities that may emerge.

Types of Technical Analysis

The two major types of technical analysis which are chart patterns and technical (statistical) indicators.

Chart Patterns

Stock chart patterns are important trading tools to incorporate into your technical analysis technique.

A chart pattern is necessary for everyone, from beginners to experts, because it aids in the identification of market trends and the prediction of market moves. Chart patterns can be used to a variety of financial markets, including Forex, stocks, commodities, and more.

The use of chart patterns is based on the opinions or expertise of individual traders with technical analysis. By examining specific patterns, the trader or investor tries to find support and resistance levels on a chart..

- These patterns supported by psychological factors can predict the direction of a price movement, follow a breakout or breakdown from a particular price level and period.

- A breakout from resistance could lead to a significant, voluminous upward movement.

- For instance, an ascending triangle chart pattern is a bullish pattern that reflects a significant resistance level.

Technical Indicators

Having data points plotted on your chart, much like a meterologist explaining weather patterns, can undoubtedly aid you in determining which way stock values are headed. You will, however, require a more thorough and exhaustive analysis of the facts accessible to you. Normally, conducting these analyses would take time, but now that technical indicators are available on your trading platforms, you can process and analyze everything very quickly. Moving averages, which are dynamic lines connecting each period's closing price, are examples of technical indicators that can be used to track trends. The majority of trading platforms allow users to manually build trendlines on the platforms. As previously said, based on the time window you are trading, your trendline may be different. Another thing that influences your trendlines is your starting point.

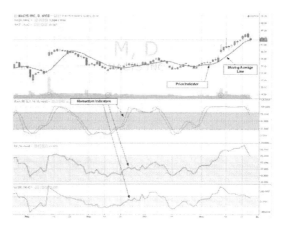

Types of Indicators

Below are some of the Types of Technical Indicators

Price/Volatility Indicators

Price indicators are used to determine price-related information such as support and resistance levels, as well as price trends. They're usually presented and tracked in the pricing area of your chart, which is usually found close to the top. Candlesticks/bars/lines, Ichimoku clouds, moving averages, pivot points, point and figure, Renko, and three-line break are some examples of price indicators. Other tools include trendlines and channels that can be drawn manually or automatically.

Momentum Indicators

The term "momentum indicators" refers to indicators that assess a stock's velocity, such as overbought and oversold levels. Simple momentum indicators are pre-programmed on almost all charting and trading platforms. These indicators are designed to assist you in properly timing your entry and exit prices. When momentum indicators indicate oversold or overbought momentum, such as a stochastic topping and falling back under the 80 band, you can avoid following prices by using good timing.

Price is important; however, understanding how price levels are determined is also vital. Commodity Channel Index (CCI), Stochastic, and Relative Strength Index (RSI) are some of the most commonly utilized indicators for determining momentum. You should be able to generate effective entry and exit signals when you combine a price and momentum indicator on your stock chart.

Trend Indicators

Averaging is used to provide a baseline for Trend Indicators, which are used to measure the direction and strength of a trend. A bullish trend is defined as price moving above the average, while a bearish trend is defined as price moving below the average. Moving averages, moving averages convergence divergence (MACD), and parabolic stop and reverse (Parabolic SAR) are some of the technical indicators employed.

Volume Indicator

Based on averaging or smoothing raw quantity, volume indicators are used to gauge the strength of a trend or confirm a trade direction. Keep in mind that the strongest trend is seen when volume is high. Increased trading activity results in large price swings. The Chaikin oscillator, On-Balance-Volume (OBV), and Volume Rate of Change are all common indicators.

Successful traders combine the use of the correct technical indicators with smart and disciplined money management abilities to arrive at highly probable set-ups and triggers.

Categories of Technical Indicators

All technical indicator falls into one of two categories. They are either lagging or leading indicators.

Here's a breakdown of some of the ones mentioned in this chapter.

An Overview of Bull and Bear Market

There are a few reasons why these two animals were picked as the symbols to signify substantial stock market events. Most interestingly, both animals attack their opponents. That provides an accurate picture of what occurs in the market.

The bull is one of the most powerful creatures on the planet. The bull attacks by thrusting its horn forward from the bottom to the top. If you've ever watched cowboys play with a bull, you've probably noticed how the bull tries to get them off its back and onto the ground. When the rider is knocked on the ground, the bull uses its horn to attack him from below. The plan is to pick up and hurl its prey. Even when the victim is still, the animal continues to do so. A rising market is regarded as a "Bullish" market because of the surge from bottom to top.

The bear, on the other hand, attacks from the top down. A powerful animal that injures its prey by using its weight, fangs, or claws to tear them apart. When the bear comes face to face with its target, it stands on two feet and to appear very large, then roars powerfully and begins shredding the victim from top to bottom. The term "Bearish" refers to a market that is dropping or sinking from top to bottom.

The names "bulls" and "bears" are frequently used in the stock market and investment sector to describe market conditions. These terms refer to how the stock market is performing in general. That is, whether their value is increasing (appreciation) or decreasing (depreciation). The direction of the market has a significant impact on your portfolio as a trader or investor. As a result, you must comprehend how each of these marketplaces affects your investment and trading approach.

Bull vs. Bear Market

Markets increase when market conditions are excellent and the economy is generally positive, and the market is said to be in a bull market when this is true. In contrast, when the economy is retreating and dreary, most stock prices begin to collapse, and prices begin to decline in value, the market is said to be bearish, and the market is described as such.

A bearish market has the potential to climb persistently. In other words, during a bull market, the price of stocks continues to rise in a steady and sustainable manner. During a bullish market, investors and traders alike have faith that the market will continue to rise in a sustainable manner over time. In this case, the country's economy is in a strong position and performing well, particularly if the number of people employed is high.

A bear market, on the other hand, is characterized by consistent declines. Bearish markets are defined as those that have declined by at least 20% from recent highs. Stock prices continue to fall during a bear market as investors lose faith in the market and sell their holdings in order to avoid additional declines in the market. The general state of the economy is grim during a bear market; the economy slows down, and unemployment rises as a result of more firms laying off their employees. The great depression of 1926 and the 2018 bearish market are notable bearish periods in the stock market history.

Features of Bull and Bear Markets

While the direction of stock prices identifies bullish and bearish conditions, there are other supporting characteristics that traders and investors should be informed about.

Demand and Supply of Securities

In a bullish market, the demand for stocks is typically greater than the supply of stocks available. More investors are willing to purchase additional stock, but the supply is limited due to the unwillingness of stockholders to sell their holdings. This will eventually result in higher stock prices as investors become increasingly willing to pay higher prices for the limited number of available stocks.

In a bear market, the sentiment is the polar opposite of the previous one. Because of the gloomy nature of the market, there are more sellers than buyers on the market at the moment. In this environment, the availability of stocks greatly exceeds demand, causing stock prices to continue to fall further in value.

Investor Psychology

Investor psychology is defined as the way in which investors perceive and ultimately react to a situation. To put it another way, the investor's frame of mind. The psychology and attitudes of investors, it turns out, do have a role in determining whether the stock market will grow or depreciate.

The performance of the stock market and the mindsets of investors are both influenced by one another. For example, investors will be more willing to join in the stock market if they believe they would profit from it.

In a bearish market, the general mood of the market is negative. Negative sentiment indicates that investors are losing trust in the stock market and are shifting their funds out of the market to safer havens such as fixed deposits until the conditions in the market are improved. This move results in a general additional reduction in the price of commodities as well as a decrease in the outflow of funds.

Change in Economic Activity

Because the companies whose stock is traded on the stock market are key players in the larger economy, the stock market and the general economy are inextricably tied to one another.

A bear market is associated with a weak and deteriorating economic environment. Firms will struggle to generate profits if customers do not spend enough, and if businesses do not make profits, they will be forced to lay off some of their employees. Additionally, their inability to turn a profit has a negative impact on the market value of its shares.

In a bull market, on the other side, the opposite occurs. There is more money to spend, and when this occurs, firms prosper and their stock prices rise, resulting in a thriving economy for all.

It is critical for a trader to be aware of the current trend in the stock market. You may make a good profit in both bullish and bearish markets if you use the appropriate combination of technical indicators. The most important thing to remember is to avoid going against the grain. You will be able to distinguish between a bullish and bearish market in its early stages if you use technical analysis and indicators to your advantage.

Chapter Two

Chapter 2

Candlestick Basics

Basics of Candlestick Chart in Technical Analysis

When we first heard the name, we pondered how a candlestick is important to my trade because we were thinking of the candlestick that lights up the room. Well, you might not be too far off the mark if you think that way. So, what exactly is a candlestick in the context of stock chart trading?

A Quick History of Candlesticks

Using the candlesticks as a technical tool to analyze rice futures prices dates back to 1600, when the Japanese first used it to trade rice futures. A candlestick was used to trade futures in 1700, and Munehisa Homma was

one among the traders who employed it. He found that, despite the connection between demand and supply of rice, the futures market was equally influenced by traders' emotions, greed, and fear, as well as by the price of rice. He came to the realization that there could be a significant gap between the value and the price of rice. The concept of measuring the emotion of the market served as the foundation for the development of candlestick analysis.

The opening and closing prices of a stock are highlighted in candlestick charts over time. Candlesticks are simple to comprehend and employ for the most part, making it 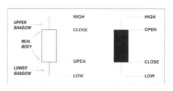 easier for a novice to grasp bar analysis and for a seasoned trader to gain a new viewpoint.

Let's get acquainted with the candlestick signs and what they mean;

- Open: The Opening price

- High: The high of the day

- Low: the low of the day

- Close: the closing price

- Real body: the range between the open and close

The body's colors reflect how the struggle between the buyers and the sellers played out;

- A true white body indicates that the closing price was higher than the opening price. A white body indicates that the market is bullish, indicating that it is a buyers' market. The greater the length of the body, the more bullish it is. A lengthy white candlestick indicates that the closing price was significantly higher than the opening, indicating a strong purchasing market.

- A true black body indicates that the closing price was less than the opening price. A bearish or sellers' market is indicated by a black body. The more bearish the body, the longer it is. A lengthy black bar indicates that the closing price was below the open and close to the low, which is difficult to see on a conventional bar but obvious on a candlestick chart. It also denotes the seller's domination in the session.

What happens if the opening and closing prices are nearly identical? This form indicates that with that candlestick, you will be unable to distinguish between supply and demand. As a result, you should refrain from trading that stock on the basis of that candlestick.

How to Read Candlestick Chart

Trading information provided by candlestick charts is frequently used by both new and experienced traders due to the wide range of trading information they provide and the distinctive style that makes it simple to interpret and read them.

This trade instrument was created several centuries ago and is still in use today in the Japanese rice market. The lines that emerge from the top and bottom of the rectangle give the shape the name candlestick, which is more appropriate. The shape is similar to that of a candlestick with a wick. The wick-like lines, on the other hand, were referred to as "shadows" by Japanese market observers.

As previously stated, each candlestick is communicating with you, and if you understand what they are saying, your trading experience will be more rewarding. For example, each candlestick has an open, high, low, and closing price for the time period you choose to trade on it. As a result, if you choose a time frame of five minutes, a new candlestick will be made every five minutes, and each of these sticks can be taken to represent something significant. When compared to other candles on an intraday chart, this candle's upper body open and close prices are every five minutes, rather than every daily trading session. Additionally, the candlestick will show you the current price as it forms, whether the price has moved up or down over the course of the time frame, as well as the price high and low ranges for that time frame, among other things.

Open Price

The open price is shown by the top or bottom of the candlestick, depending on whether the stock moved higher or lower during the given time frame. Alternatively, if the price closes higher than it opened due to a bullish trend,

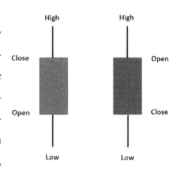

the open is represented by the bottom of the body, and the close is represented by the top of the body. Alternatively, if the price closes lower than it opened due to a downward trend, the open is represented by the top of the candlestick (without the wick), and the close is represented by the bottom of the candlestick. When a candlestick closes higher on a colored stock chart platform, it is more typically filled in as a green or white candlestick, whereas candlesticks that close lower are more often filled in as a black or red candlestick, respectively.

High Price

The high price on a candlestick period can be identified by the top of the shadow or tail above the body of the candlestick. When the open or close price for a time period is the highest price for that time period, an upper shadow will not appear.

Low Price

A low price for a stock in a given period is indicated by the tail below the body or the bottom of the shadow. If the open or close is the lowest price, there will be no lower shadow formed.

Close Price

This is the most recent price exchanged within the candlestick's time period, as shown by the top (green or white) or bottom (red or black) of the body.

Based on price movements for the stock, candlestick prices are constantly moving up and down in form. Until the candle's time frame expires, the open remains open. The high and low prices, on the other hand, will continue to fluctuate due to volatility. The color of the candlestick is also likely to alter as it forms. For example, if the current price rises above the opening and then falls below, it can change from green to red. As one candlestick's time period comes to a conclusion, the last price becomes the closing price, and a new one begins to form

Price Direction

You can tell the direction and movement of a price by looking at the color and position. If the candlestick is green or white, it indicates that the price closed higher than it did at the beginning of the opening. When a new candlestick is added, it will be placed higher to the right of the previous candlestick, unless it is shorter or a different color than the preceding candlestick. The price closed below its opening when the candlestick is red or black, and the candlestick will be situated lower to the right of the one before it, with the exception of when it is shorter and its color is different from the candlestick before it.

Price Range

The upper body of a candle is the distance between the top of the higher shadow and the bottom of the lower shadow, which represents the range within which the stock's price changed over time. By subtracting the lower price from the higher price, you can find the range.

Interpreting Patterns

After you've learned the fundamentals of the candlestick chart and what it represents, you can start looking for different patterns on the chart. Distinct candle lengths indicate different trends, and all traders should learn how to read these patterns.

Here are some candlesticks and interpretations that may be useful in the future:

Short White Candlestick

The short white candlestick indicates a weak buying demand, with little or no price movement, as indicated by the short white candlestick. The candlestick can be distinguished by its color and size, which are both white and little. The white body is anticipated to be small, al-

Short White Candlestick

though the lengths and shadows are largely irrelevant in this case. As a result, relying on this one candlestick to draw a bullish conclusion about the company is not sufficient because it is only valid for a limited time period. You must take into account the candles surrounding it in order to make an informed choice on market direction.

White Candlestick

This candlestick illustrates the regular buying pressure that occurred during the time period. It also demonstrates that prices moved well from the opening to the closing of the session, and that the bulls maintained control throughout. The average length and color of

White Candlestick

this candle, which is white, distinguish it from others. The length of the white candle body should be of average length, however the length of the shadow is not vital to evaluate.

In this case, you can't rely on a single candlestick to determine whether or not a market is bullish because you're only looking at a stick for a short length of time. It could indicate either the continuation of a trend or its reversal. To get a clearer sense of the market's direction, additional supporting candles will be required.

Long White Candlestick

The long white candlestick, like the white candlestick, indicates that there was reasonably strong purchasing pressure throughout the period from open to closure, and that the bulls were aggressive during the period from open to close. The candlestick's body is made of white

Long White Candlestick

ceramic and is quite lengthy. In addition, when compared to other candlesticks, the white body of this one is longer.

Although this is a bullish candlestick, it is still important to analyze its location in relation to the larger technical picture as a whole. It is possible that this is a signal of reversal, indicating that prices have achieved a support level after a protracted period of decline. If this candlestick appears after a long rally, it may suggest that the market has become too bullish and that prices have reached volatile highs.

White Marubozu

This lengthy white candlestick with no shadows indicates that the market is extremely bullish. The candlestick signifies extreme bullishness and is distinguished by having a lengthy white body with no shadows on either end and a body that is white. When compared to the other candlesticks on the chart, its white body should be slightly longer.

White Marubozu

In the case of a white Marubozu, it means that the beginning price is equal to or lower than the day's low and that the closing price is equal or higher than the period's high. Additionally, it demonstrates that the bulls have complete control over the market action during the duration. In addition, it means that prices rose at the start of the time and remained elevated throughout, as seen by the long white candlestick with no shadows.

While this is unquestionably a positive indication, it is also necessary to assess its significance in the context of the overall technical picture. It might be a potential reversal, indicating that prices have reached support levels following a prolonged decline, according to the chart. If this candlestick appears after a long and big rally, it may indicate that the market has become too bullish and that prices have risen to dangerously high levels. Please keep in mind that different candlesticks can provide a more reliable indication of market direction and a realistic view of the market.

White Closing Marubozu

This candlestick begins with a bit of shadow and a solid white body, indicating extreme bullishness. The upper body of this candle is longer than others, with an opening shadow but no closing shadow.

White Closing Marubozu

A white closing Marubozu depicts how buyers dominated the period in comparison to others, as shown by the upper body price action of this candle from the start to the end of the period in question. The period began with prices falling slightly, forming the lower shadow, followed by a strong rebound that took prices past the opening and continued until the finish, with closing prices equal to the day's high. In summary, the bulls started slowly but became more bold in their purchases as the period progressed.

Bullish dominance is indicated by this candlestick. The larger technical picture, on the other hand, may indicate the possibility of a turnaround and suggest that prices have peaked at their support level following a long decline. It's common after a long significant rally and therefore can indicate excessively bullishness and prices that are dangerously high.

This candlestick has a lengthy white body with an upper shadow but no lower shadow, indicating that the stock is extremely bullish. When compared to the other bodies on the chart, the white body should be longer. Only a shadow at the top differentiates it.

White Opening Marubozu

An opening in the white Marubozu indicates that the bulls controlled the market activity from the beginning to the end of the period. The period began on a high note, and the price continued to rise following a lengthy rally, resulting in the long white body with no shadow. The prices, however, did not close at the period's high, which is why we have the upper shadow.

This candlestick is bullish for the most part, but its position within the larger technical picture is critical. A Bullish Belt Hold Pattern may signify a reversal after prices have achieved a support level after a protracted rally. This type of candle appears after a long and critical surge and may indicate that the market has become overly bullish and that prices have reached dangerously high levels.

Short Black Candlestick

This small black candlestick indicates weak selling pressure and restricted price movement for the time period. The body of the candlestick is black and small, and the length of the shadows is unimportant. Because it just

Short Black Candlestick

displays the price level of a single period on the chart, you shouldn't rely on this candlestick to make negative judgments. It could be a continuation or reversal of a trend. Before you can draw a more secure conclusion about the market's direction, you must analyze other candlesticks.

Long Black Candlestick

This candlestick is dark and lengthy, indicating a slight increase in selling pressure. It also shows that prices dropped dramatically between the open and close times. The sellers were more aggressive around this time. The length of this candlestick's shadows is unimportant.

Long Black Candlestick

Although the broader technical picture of this candlestick must be taken into account, it is primarily bearish. This could also be a sign of a reversal, indicating that after a protracted rally, the price has encountered a resistance level. After an extended decline, this candlestick may appear, indicating that the bears have overpowered the bulls or panic selling. It could also be a last-ditch attempt at a selloff before the bulls take control. Still, this isn't a stand-alone candlestick; for a more accurate prediction, you'll need further information from the surrounding candle.

Black Marubozu

This candlestick has no shadows, it's long, and has a black body, indicating an extreme bearish position for the timeframe in question. When the beginning price equals the day's high and the closing price equals the day's low, this sort of candlestick is formed. It

Black Marubozu

means that the sellers were in charge of price movement from the beginning to the end of the period. Prices continued to fall uninterrupted as the era began, forming a long black candlestick with no shadows. Though a larger perspective is still required, this candlestick is primarily a negative indicator. It could, however, be a hint of a possible reversal, indicating that prices have struck a resistance level following a protracted rally.

After an extended downward trend, this style of candlestick may signify panic, a bearish takeover, or a final selloff before the bulls reclaim control. This isn't, however, a stand-alone candlestick. For a better prediction, you'll need more information from the surrounding candle.

Black Opening Marubozu

This candlestick with a long black body has a lower shadow but no higher shadow, indicating that the stock is extremely bearish. When compared to the other bodies on the chart, the black body should be longer. Only a shadow at the bottom distinguishes it.

Black Opening Marubozu

An aperture in the dark From the beginning of the period through the end, the bears dominated the price activity, according to Marubozu. The period began on a low, and after a big extended rise, the price continued to decline, resulting in the long black body with no shadow. However, because the prices did not close at the period's low, the shadow is lower.

This candlestick is bearish for the most part, but its position within the larger technical picture is critical. A Bearish Belt Hold Pattern may signify a reversal when prices have reached a resistance level after an extended drop. This type of candle appears after a long and significant rally and may indicate that the market is overly bearish and that prices are dangerously low.

Black Closing Marubozu

This candlestick begins with a sliver of shadow and a completely black body, denoting extreme bearishness. The lower body of this candle is longer than others, with an opening shadow but no shadow at the closing or bottom. A black finish From the beginning through

Black Closing Marubozu

the end of the period in question, Marubozu explains how sellers controlled the price motion. Prices began to rise slightly, forming the upper shadow, followed by a significant decrease that drove prices below the opening and lasted until the end of the period, with closing prices equal to the day's low. In summary, the bears started cautiously but became more bold in their purchase as the period progressed.

Bearish dominance is indicated by this candlestick. The larger technical picture, on the other hand, may indicate the possibility of a reversal and suggest that after a long run, prices are at severe lows and resistance levels. It's common after a long critical downturn and could indicate excessive bearishness and that prices are dangerously low.

Doji

The length and color of this candlestick are null because it's a result of indecisiveness in price action for the period under review. Also, note that other candlesticks with close-to-zero body and length, with either white or black body colors, are called Doji.

Doji

Doji is a particularly interesting candlestick because it represents a tug of war between buys and sellers with no clear winner. It shows how prices have moved above and below the opening during the period; however, the session closed either precisely how it opened or close to the opening. It's a standoff. It shows neither the bulls nor the bear had the momentum to gain control of the period and that a turning point could be looming.

On its own, it provides more information and features other patterns as vital elements. To interpret it accurately, you need to see the candlestick before or after. If a Doji shows up after a long white candlestick, it means the buying pressure may be growing weaker. On the other hand, a Doji after a long black candlestick could mean the selling pressure is thinning out. In essence, the Doji tells you that the buyers and sellers are evenly matched, and a change in trend may lurk. However, Doji alone is not enough to identify a reversal; further confirmation is needed.

The relevance of Doji as a signal is somewhat comparable and depends on the characteristics of the market. It only calls for attention when it's a rare appearance on the chart during a session, but where several other Doji are forming here and there, it becomes of little importance and carries negligible value.

White Spinning Top

This type of candlestick looks like a Doji and should be interpreted as one when it appears. The primary features include a tiny white body, an upper longer shadow, and a lower longer shadow.

Although a small reflection of a bullish dominance during the pe-

White Spinning Top

riod, it's actually a tussle between the bears and the bulls. Prices moved higher and sharply lower, or vice versa then closed above the opening price, which created the tiny white body. The length of the shadow is not essential, but the small white body, compared with the shadows, makes it a spinning top.

Observing this type of candlestick formation after a long rally or after a long white candlestick may signify weakness in the bullish move and a likely interruption in the trend.

Like other lone candlesticks patterns, the white spinning top has low reliability. It only tells the story of the event of that period which can be interrupted both as a continuation or a change in direction. You need to use this candlestick along with others to form a reliable opinion on a trend.

Black Spinning Top

This type of candlestick looks like a Doji and should be interpreted as one when it appears. The primary features include a tiny black body, an upper longer shadow, and a lower longer shadow.

Black Spinning Top

Although a small reflection of a bearish dominance during the period, it's actually a tussle between the bears and the bulls. Prices moved lower and then sharply higher, or vice versa, then closed above the opening price, creating the tiny black body. The length of the shadow is not important, but the small black body, compared with the shadows, makes it a spinning top.

When you observe the formation of this type of candlestick after a long fall or after a long black candlestick, it may be a sign of a weakness in the bearish move and a likely interruption in the trend.

Like other lone candlesticks patterns, the black spinning top has low reliability. It only tells the story of the event of that period which can be interrupted both as a continuation or a change in direction. You need to use this candlestick along with others to form a reliable opinion on a trend.

Four Price Doji

The features of the four price
Doji include;   Four Price Doji

- Null body length

- Colorless body   —

- Null upper and lower shadows

- Open, close, high, and low prices are the same although the period.

Only when all four price components are identical does this candlestick develop, making it an unique sight to behold. That is, there was no movement in the price throughout that trading session. This occurs when there is complete and utter uncertainty between the bulls and bears about the direction of the market. It occurs when there is little momentum, little volume, or when the data sources fail to disclose any prices other than the closing price of the previous day.

The four-price Doji, like other candlesticks, is untrustworthy on its own, and this is no exception. In reality, it just represents a period of hesitation. When it appears on your chart only once, the four-price Doji, like all other Doji, only makes sense in that situation. Their importance decreases in proportion to the number of Doji, and vice versa.

Long Legged Doji

This Doji has no body, but its up-
per and lower shadows are longer.   Long Legged Doji
The long-legged Doji is unique in
that it indicates that prices traded well above and below the opening price for the time, but that they
closed at or near the opening price.
It may also be deduced that, despite
the great volatility and excitement over the period, the price finished
the same way it opened. It's an obvious sign of market hesitation, but
it gets significant when it appears at the peak or bottom of a trend.

Umbrella

The umbrella has unique fea-
tures, which include;   Umbrella

- The length of the body is
  close to null or null and
  colorless

- There is no upper shadow

- It has a long lower shadow

The interpretation of an umbrella is that the bears dominated and
controlled the price movement for the duration, but that toward the
end of the period, the bulls showed up and pushed prices up to close
at the same opening or at the high for the period, as indicated by the
dotted line.

A bullish reversal could be signaled by the appearance of an umbrella after a protracted decline, such as the appearance of a long black
candlestick, or by the appearance of an umbrella around a support

level. When an umbrella appears after a long uptrend, following a long white candlestick, or when it is observed at a resistance level, it may indicate a bearish trend reversal on the other hand. In both cases, you will require confirmation in either the bullish or bearish direction.

Inverted Umbrella

The umbrella has unique features, which include;

Inverted Umbrella

- The length of the body is close to null or null and colorless

- There is no lower shadow

- It has a long upper shadow

This pattern indicates that the bulls dominated and controlled price movement for most of the period, but then the bears appeared and pushed prices lower until they reached the same opening price or the lowest price for the period at the close of trading.

It is possible that the inverted umbrella may appear after a long uptrend, such as after a white and black candlestick, or that it will appear near a support level, signaling the beginning of a bearish reversal. In contrast, if an inverted umbrella appears after a protracted decline, following a long black candlestick, or when it appears at a resistance level, it could indicate a positive reversal in the market. In both cases, you will require confirmation in either the bullish or bearish direction.

Chapter Three

Chapter 3

Bullish and Bearish Patterns

C andlesticks are one of the most important tools in the technical analysis toolbox. With candlesticks, you can quickly determine information about the price of a stock just on a few bars of information. When it comes to the fluctuation in the price of a stock, they have plenty of stories to share with you.

In this chapter, we'll talk about bullish and bearish patterns, as well as how to recognize them by looking at your candlesticks and chart. First and foremost, let us recall the characteristics of a candlestick that we discussed earlier.

- **The body,** which represents the open-to-close range.

- **The wick** or **shadow** indicates the intra-day high and low.

- **The color**, which reveals the direction of market movement – a green (or white) body indicates a price increase, while a red (or black) body shows a price decrease.

When you look at the patterns generated by each candlestick, you may use them to identify important support and resistance levels in the stock you are trading. There are various patterns that the candlesticks form, and each pattern tells a different tale. Some of these indicators provide information regarding a balance between bulls and bears in terms of purchasing and selling pressure. While some believe that markets are continuing in their current direction, others believe that they are undecided.

As previously said, we are primarily concerned with bullish and bearish candlestick patterns. As a result, we will be looking at six different forms of these patterns for each of them.

Six Bullish Candlestick Pattern

A bullish pattern is most often formed following a market downturn or bearish trend. It has the potential to suggest a reversal in price movement. Whether using the candlestick, some indicators can help you determine when it is time to go long in anticipation of a bullish reversal.

Hammer

When a downward trend is in full swing, this candlestick pattern is generated with a short body and a long shadow at the bottom. A hammer candlestick pattern indicates that, despite the fact that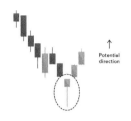

there was selling pressure during the interval in question, the bulls outperformed the bears in pushing the price back upwards. Bull bodies are painted in a variety of colors depending on the platform, but in this case, the bulls' green bodies are a sign of strength.

Inverse Hammer

 Another bullish pattern identical to the one above. The key distinction is that the upper shadow is longer, but the lower shadow is shorter and has a smaller body. It's a sign that purchasing pressure has increasingly surpassed selling pressure. It signifies that both buyers and sellers contended throughout the era, but the buyers prevailed, resulting in a price increase at the end of the period. The purchasers are getting ready to seize control, according to Inverse.

Bullish Engulfing

Two candlesticks make up this pattern. The first is a bearish candle with a small red body that has been completely enveloped by a larger bullish candle that has appeared di-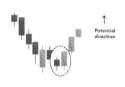

rectly next to it. It means that, despite the fact that the second opens lower than the first, the bullish market pushes the price higher, resulting in a clear bullish victory.

Piercing Line

Another twin candlestick pattern, this one with a long red candle followed by a long green candle.
As the price rises up to or over the
previous time's mid-point, it's an
indication of intense buying pressure.

Morning Star

The morning star candlestick
pattern, as its name suggests, is a
sign of hope or a new day after a long downward trend. It's a
three-candlestick arrangement with

one short-bodied candle sandwiched between a long red and a green
candle. As the market gaps on both open and close, the "star" will
typically have no overlap over the longer bodies.

Three White Soldiers

The bullish pattern of the three
white soldiers appears on three different time frames. It is made up
of three successive bullish candles
(green or white) with short shadows, each of which opens and closes higher than the previous one. This type of signal occurs after a
significant negative move and suggests that the bulls are engaging in
aggressive buying.

Six Bearish Candlestick Pattern

Bearish candlestick patterns are frequently generated following a bullish surge and are used to indicate the presence of a point of resistance. In this period, investors feel apprehensive about the continuation of the bullish movement, prompting them to open sell positions in order to profit from the price decline that is taking place.

Hanging Man

In bullish patterns, this is the inverse of the hammer. The main distinction is that it appears at the end of an uptrend in the form of a long shadow underneath a little upper  body. During the day, there was a large sell-off, but purchasers were able to bring the price back up. The significant sell-off indicates a weakness in bullish buying and the emergence of bears.

Shooting Star

The shooting star is the inverted hammer in reverse, and it is frequently seen near the end of an uptrend. It has a short upper shadow and a small body. Frequently, the  market will open with a little gap, rally to an intra-day high, and then close at a price somewhat higher than the opening.

Bearish Engulfing

At the end of a bullish run, this bearish pattern appears. It's a two-candlestick pattern, with the first having a small green body with

a tiny shadow and the second being consumed by a long sale candle. With price movement slowing, it's a sign of a bullish trend culminating. This is also a hint of an oncoming reversal, which might lead to a bearish takeover. The stronger the trend is projected to be, the lower the second candle is.

Evening Star

This is a three-candlestick pat-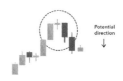
tern that resembles a bullish morn-
ing star in appearance. It's a small
candle that looks like a cross,
wedged between two long green
and enormous red candlesticks. It's a sign of a reversal in the positive trend that had been in place up to that time. When the third candlestick wipes out the gains of the first candle, this is another evidence of the strength of the reversal.

Three Black Crows

Three consecutive lengthy bear-
ish candles with short or non-ex-
istent shadows make up the three
black crow candlestick pattern.
Each session begins at a same price
as the previous one, but with each candle, the selling pressure lowers the price lower. Because the sellers have taken control over the last three periods, traders perceive these patterns as a reversal and the start of a bearish downturn.

Dark Cloud Cover

A bearish reversal is indicated by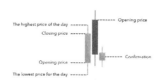
this candlestick pattern. It casts a
cloud on the optimism of the previous day. It's made up of two can-

dlesticks: a red candle that opens
above the previous green body and closes below its midpoint, and
a green candle that opens above the previous green body and closes
below its midway. This is a strong indication that the bears have gained
control of the session and are driving the market lower. If the candle's
shadow is short, it indicates that a downturn is unmistakably in effect.

Chapter Four

Chapter 4

Stock Trading Chart Patterns

Everyone who is interested in trading, from beginners to pros, and especially those who wish to incorporate technical analysis into their trading strategy, must understand chart patterns and how to use them more effectively in order to set up trades. Chart patterns provide a more accurate picture of the stock market and assist you in making more accurate predictions about it. In addition to using chart patterns to analyze the stock market, you can use chart patterns to analyze the Forex market, commodities markets, and other markets.

The chart patterns that we will be studying in this chapter are some of the more straightforward to recognize and understand. Those are some of the most prevalent patterns to keep an eye out for while developing a technical analysis plan for your trades. In addition, they are the most fundamental chart pattern for the stock market. If you can comprehend what they are saying, you will have gone a great step closer to realizing your ambition of becoming a stock trader.

Ascending Triangle

Bullish "continuation" patterns like this one imply that a breakout is imminent when the triangle lines are closed. First, draw a horizontal line at the resistance point and then 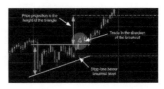 a vertical one (the uptrend line) at the support points to arrive at a recognizable pattern. You can see the projected height of the triangle in the chart above, which suggests that if you have a good entry and are trading in the direction of the breakout, the price could rise. The breakout point is a secure spot to place your stop-loss.

Descending Triangle

Because they show a downward trend, ascending triangles are the inverse of ascending triangles, and hence represent a bearish market in the same way that descending tri- 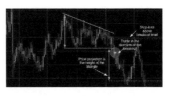 angles are. As can be seen in this example, the support line is horizontal and the resistance line is falling, indicating the probability of a bearish breakout trend.

Start by positioning your trade in the direction of the decline, with your stop loss a few points above the breakout level. The intensity of the projected price movement can be seen in the chart to the right.

Symmetrical Triangle

In the case of symmetrical triangles, two trend lines begin to converge, signaling the commence-
ment of a breakout; this time,
the breakout could be upward or

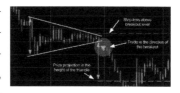

downward. The upward breakout is used to form the support line,
while the downward breakout is used to draw the resistance line. Although the trend may wind up in either direction, it normally follows
the market's current trend.

The market began with a negative trend, with the price forecast
equal to the height of the arrow and the stop-loss put slightly above
the breakout level, as seen in the chart.

Pennant

Pennants are two lines that meet
at a fixed place, unlike symmetrical
triangles. After a big bullish or negative market action, these lines are
formed when traders take a breath

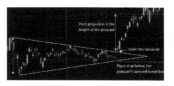

and allow the price to stabilize before the trend restarts in the same
direction. You can see how the lines meet at some point on the chart,
and how the trend restarts after a small halt. Trade the breakout while
keeping an eye on the price estimate.

Flag

The support and resistance lines
run parallel until the breakout
occurs on the flag chart, which
is formed like a falling rectangle.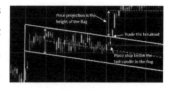
When a breakout occurs, it usually
happens in the opposite direction of the trendlines. It's an indicator
of a trend reversal.

Wedge

Because the breakout often runs
counter to the market's current
trend, this is frequently a reversal
pattern. Wedge patterns show a tight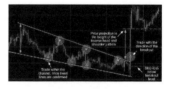
price movement between support
and resistance, and they can be either bullish or bearish. In contrast to
triangles, wedges do not feature horizontal trend lines. Bullish trend
lines or bearish trend lines can be used to identify them.

A bullish wedge will see the price break through the resistance line,
while a bearish wedge will see the price break through the support line.

As you can see from the chart, after verifying the trend line, you can
trade within the channels, and when a breakout occurs, you can trade
in the direction of the breakout. Your stop loss should be placed below
the breakout point.

Double Bottom

The double bottom chart pattern has the shape of the letter "W,"
which indicates that it has attempt-
ed to break through the support level twice but has failed. Because it

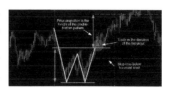

clearly depicts a reversal in trend following a failed attempt to break
support levels, this is another reversal chart pattern to a bullish trend
in the making. It is important to observe the trend lines, price predictions, and suggested stop-loss levels on the chart.

Double Top

In the case of a double bottom, it
is the opposite side. In this instance,
the chart pattern resembles the letter
M, and a negative trend begins when
prices have failed to break through

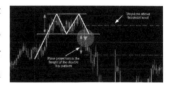

the resistance level twice. Prices move in the direction of support levels
before resuming a downward trend that breaks the support line.

According to the chart, the initial trend was bullish, and the price
failed to break through resistance twice before reverting and beginning
a new bearish trend.

Head and shoulders

The head and shoulder chart
patterns are designed to anticipate
the reversal of a bear market that
is currently in progress. This may
be distinguished by the presence of
two lesser peaks, one to the right and the other to the left of a higher
resistance level, and the fact that all three prices have fallen back to
the same levels. The trend will eventually break out as a bearish trend
as a result of this development. In the chart above, you can see that
the bullish trend changed into a bearish trend after many attempts to
break through the barrier level were unsuccessful. You can view the
price levels of the projects as well as the potential profits. Don't forget
to place your stop loss a little above the price levels that marked the
breakout.

Rounding Top or Bottom

The rounding bottom or cup
chart pattern is frequently used to
indicate an upward trend, whereas
the rounding top chart pattern is
used to indicate a downward trend.
When the U shape is formed, you can set up a trade to buy at the
midpoint by taking advantage of the trend that follows as it breaks
through the resistance. The chart above shows you where you should
begin a trade, how much money you could make, and where you
should place your stop loss.

Cup and Handle

The cup and handle pattern is a well-known chart pattern that suggests an upward trend in the stock market. In terms of appearance, it is quite similar to the Rounding Top and Bottom de-

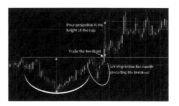

sign, but it has a smaller U shape that is more reminiscent of the handle of a cup. That handle, which might seem like a pennant or a flag pattern at times, indicates that the market is obviously in an upward trend until it finally forms when it does.

Place your stop-loss order below the candlestick that appears just prior to the breakout price, and set your trade to take profit based on the size of your projects and the height of the cup.

What is a Breakout

In practically all of the chart patterns we've studied thus far, we've mentioned "breakouts" at least a couple of times, which you may have noticed. So, what is a stock breakout and how does it occur? A breakout in the price of a particular company on the stock market represents a trading opportunity that novices and even experienced traders should be aware of in order to take advantage of it when it presents itself. In the financial markets, there are hundreds of traders whose sole strategy is to trade the breakout.

In the case of a negative trend, a breakout happens when a stock price finally moves beyond a support level that it has previously struggled to breach, and when a stock price moves above a resistance level in the case of a bullish trend. Understanding how to detect and start trading breakouts is valuable knowledge to have, and it should be acquired in conjunction with another technical tool to make yourself a well-rounded trader. Breakouts on chart patterns can be identified by reading the price action with the help of candlesticks.

Breakout Patterns

Prices are driven by the demand and supply of a certain stock, so when a breakout occurs, it simply indicates that the purchasing pressure has intensified even further, and the bulls have successfully pushed the price over the resistance price level in an uptrend. However, sellers are gaining ground on purchasers in anticipation of a bearish or negative stock breakout, and the resulting pressure has pushed stock prices above the support level.

Remember that not all breakouts will result in significant price volatility, but that every major price movement has a series of breakouts that all begin with an initial breakout in order to get the desired result. As a trader, it's critical to learn how to recognize when a breakout is likely to occur and how to capitalize on the opportunity. In addition to the chart patterns that we discussed previously, I'd like to show you one more example.

Bollinger Band Breakout

The Bollinger Band is a technical analysis approach that, when properly applied, can assist you in identifying when a stock is about to break out. Bollinger Bands are often used in conjunction with a candlestick chart to move in tandem with the prices by forming an envelope around the price. You can set the bands to be a standard deviation away from a 20-period moving average, or you can set them to any amount you choose depending on your previous trading history. The price, as expected, remains within the ranges.

When the volume of a stock is high or when the price change is significant, the bands are always far apart, both at the top and at the bottom of the chart. When volume and price movements are low, the bands will converge to the point where they are virtually touching each other's tip. Large price movements are always followed by a breakout, which occurs shortly after the quiet period. You can see in the figure below how the bands initially converge, forming a narrow pattern before breaking out and finally contributing to a doubling in stock values. An upward breakthrough happens above the Bollinger Band, which indicates the possibility of a further upward breakout.

When employing a Bollinger Band, a stop-loss order should normally be set at the lower band once the entry is completed. As the price  rises, you can increase or decrease your stop-loss as necessary.

Chapter Five

Chapter 5

Breaking Down the Charts

C onsider the following scenario: you are a trader or aspiring trader who enjoys reading stock charts, identifying trends, keeping an eye out for price resistance, and drawing trendlines to support your positions. If this is the case, it indicates that you are gradually embracing technical analysis as your preferred trading approach. Understanding the types of stock charts that are regularly used, as well as how to read them, is essential for honing your technical abilities and techniques.

Stock Chart Types

Here's a list of the four most common charts used in stock trading:

Bar Charts

By far the most used chart type is the bar chart.

The bar chart is the default chart that shows on your screen when you download or open a new trade chart. The bar chart is intended to display primary data.

- Opening price

- Closing price

- The high price of the day

- The low price of the day

A vertical line illustrates the range through a horizontal line pointing left to mark the initial price and another horizontal line pointing right to indicate the closing price when looking at a daily history.

Candlestick Charts

The candlestick charts display the same data as the bar charts, but in a different manner. The graphic is divided into two sections. The first part is the "shadow," which is a thin line at the bottom or top of the line that displays the price

range, opening, and closing for the time window you're watching. The "true body" is the part of the line that is wider. It calculates the price difference between the open and close of a trade. The true body turns green or white if the closing price is higher than the opening price. The genuine body, on the other hand, becomes red or black if the closing price is lower than the opening.

Please refer to chapter 2 for more on candlestick patterns.

Line Charts

A line chart differs from bar and candlestick charts in that it just tracks the closing price of each timeframe and connects the closes of each timeframe into a single continuous line. Some skilled traders believe that the closing price 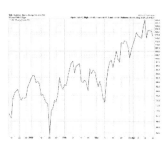 is the most important piece of information to have on a chart, and that the opening price is the least important. For these types of traders, the line chart is the only thing that matters when it comes to studying and strategizing.

Point and Figure Charts

Another chart that is different from the line chart in that it simply focuses on pricing rather than time and volume. Price rises are represented by the letter "X," whereas price decreases are represented by the letter "O." Some experts claim that by using this chart, they can more easily discern trends and reversals. The disadvantage is that, because there is no information on time or volume, it is difficult to cal-  culate how long it will take to reach your target profit using a Point and Figure chart. Because volume is not measured, it is also impossible to determine whether the market is active or in a range of prices. Every chart in technical analysis serves a specific purpose and has its own set of advantages and disadvantages. Take time to investigate each of them during your practice session so that you can identify the one that best offers you with the knowledge you need to be lucrative in the market.

Stock Chart Components

Here's a stock chart of the NASDAQ Composite with some major parts labeled for easy explanation. Let's now review stock charts and the essential features, what they mean, and how to identify them.

Chart Identification

Every chart is labeled so that you will always know what you are looking at, at any given time, before you begin trading it. Taking a look at the chart above, you'll notice that it's a chart of the $COMPAQ INDX, which represents the Nasdaq Composite Index in the upper left corner. Similarly, if the stock had been Microsoft, you would have gotten the shorter version of MSFT or Google for GOOG instead.

Summary Key

There is a brief description of the day's events on that stock presented on the chart, which is labeled 2. The index's most recent price is represented by the number 2303.54, which is displayed on the screen. You can see the word "daily" to the left of the number, which indicates that the time frame you are viewing is the "Daily" chart of the index you are looking at. Monthly, weekly, 4 hour, hour, and minute time frames are also accessible on most charts, as are other time frames. Moving averages in blue and red (50 day and 200 day) are shown below; more information on moving averages can be found further down the page. The primary goal of the summary is to provide you with a condensed version of the information about the stock you are currently examining.

Time/Period

The period is always displayed on the X-axis. From the following chart, you can see the dates from left to right, with months and days in between. The chart still can show you a shorter timeframe the shorter the time frame the more granular slice of time you are viewing. If you examine the chart on a daily time frame, for example, the chart will exhibit more time than if you view it on an hourly time period.

Moving Averages

Moving averages are types of technical analysis that help display support and resistance levels of prices action on a stock chart. The red line represents a 200-day moving average in our chart above, while the blue is the 50-day moving average.

Volume

Volume plays an important role in determining the market's momentum, depending on the type of approach you will use for your trade. Each bar represents a day on the technical indicator on the chart we're looking at. The average volume over the last 60 days is represented by the red line that runs through the tops. The longer or taller the bars are, the more stock of that particular stock was exchanged that day.

The time frame you are monitoring per time adjusts the technical indicators. In other words, if the main chart is switched to an hourly time frame, the technical indicator will change as well.

Daily Trade Range

Each red or black vertical line on the chart indicates a trading day, just like the line in volume. In other words, if you're looking at a weekly chart, each chart will show weekly data. A red bar indicates that the index's stock was lower during that time period compared to the previous day. When compared to the previous time, black bars indicate that the stock or index is at a higher level.

The Importance of Volume

The importance of volume in stock trading cannot be overstated, especially if you have chosen to rely on technical indicators as a component of your trading strategy. The number of shares or contracts traded in a certain period of time is referred to as the volume. It means that every time you purchase or sell shares, you are adding to the overall volume of that particular stock market.

In the stock market, it is not uncommon for millions of shares to be traded in a single day. For example, the S&P 500 ETF (SPY) trades an average of 75 million shares within a single trading day. Every day that the stock market is open, billions of dollars' worth of stock is exchanged between buyers and sellers. On the other hand, the stocks of tiny companies, typically referred to as "penny stocks," may only trade a few thousand shares every market session on a daily basis.

Understanding the significance of volume and how to track it will enable you to make better and more educated trading decisions in the future. Here are two of the most important reasons to use volume tracking as a trading strategy in your trade.

Support and Resistance

Consider the following scenario: you toss a pebble at a glass window, and the window may not crack or even break; even if another person joins you in throwing more stones, the window may still not feel the effect. However, if you throw a hundred pebbles and rocks of varying sizes at the same glass, the chances of it breaking increase dramatically. For example, if an investor wants to purchase 200 shares of stock at the current ask price, the impact may be minor; but, if 200 individuals request different quantities of the same stock, the stock is more likely to move, especially if the buyers outnumber the sellers.

When it comes to breaking through price levels of support and resistance, it is important to remember that volume is important in terms of quantity.

Average Daily Volume

The overall volume of a stock in a given period will help you comprehend the amount of power that stock has on a particular market or sector. Generally speaking, the bigger the volume, the greater the significance of the total meaningful time frame. When a piece of big news, such as earnings, is announced, stocks tend to trade at a higher volume than usual. Knowing how to plot the average daily volume on a stock chart provides you with valuable insight into how to detect accumulation and distribution days on the chart, which you can then use to identify momentum and predict future price moves.

It is not particularly simple to read the volume, accumulation, and dispersion of a stock chart on a computer screen. It takes a lot of practice to become proficient at something. However, once you have mastered the talent, it becomes a significant asset in terms of earning a good profit in the market.

Channels

Channels are formed when the price action in a particular stock is in a trend but seems to try to reverse. They come in three forms.

Horizontal Channels

This form of channel is referred to as a price range or a sideways trend in some circles. Essentially, they are trend lines connecting changing pivot highs and lows in

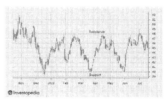

order to demonstrate that price is contained between the upper line of resistance and the lower line of support. In this situation, both buyers and sellers of the stock in question place the equal amount of pressure on the price, resulting in a sideways movement of the stock price. As a trader who has put in the necessary time and effort, you will be able to pinpoint your entry and exit points and even trade both sides.

Ascending Channels

Ascending channels are constructed by drawing two positive sloping trending lines above and below a set of resistance and support levels, and then connecting the two

lines. They are price movements between two bullish sloping parallel lines that are in close proximity. Price activity has created higher highs and higher lows, which are represented by the chart. Bullish channels of this type are most commonly used to confirm a bullish trend.

Descending Channels

Descending trendlines are formed when traders believe that the stock price is still in a bearish trend overall, despite multiple attempts by the bulls to turn the trend around. As a result, the price continues to fluctuate within the confines of the channel trendline.

It is possible to create a descending channel by connecting a parallel trend line between a stock's lower and lower lows and the lower and lower highs . The descending channel is defined by the space between the trend lines.

Another great point of entry is when the price breaks out of a channel. Here's an example of a stock chart for Fastenal (FAST) showing a descending channel.

1. The daily chart view shows how the company stock price formed a channel for four months, which can also be considered a large channel.

2. There was a breakout downwards outside the channel for two days as we saw intensified selling from the bears, but after that, the buying volume more than doubled the selling and led to a reversal back into the channel. If you had assumed a further fall when the price broke out of the channels, you would have suffered minor losses there. What happened seemed to be the effect of the news because, as we can see, the trend reversed after 48 hours and reached $40.

3. At this point, we can see how the descending channel now served as a support line at $38. That is, the previous resistance becomes support. Another buying opportunity, the price rallied off this support and up above $40.

4. We can see the resumption of the bullish trend that started at point 2 here as the stock claimed a higher high above $44 and broke out of a small base.

Channels are formed by a combination of existing trendlines and additional parallel lines. Prices will typically oscillate between the trendline and the parallel line, causing swing traders to take advantage and make some good profits.

As long as the prices remain within a range, swing traders can buy at the support price and sell when the price gets to the resistance level and vice versa.

Identifying channels successfully gives you a great advantage to get ahead of the market, and the best way to achieve this is through practice. There are several false positives to look out for in the market, so your practice period should be taken seriously.

Price Gaps

A gap on a stock chart is a point of discontinuity where the prices rise from the previous day's closing price without any indication of trading activity in between. When a large piece of news has an impact on a stock near the end of a trading session, this is known as a gap. To put it simply, a price gap occurs when a stock closes at a given price, such as 4 PM EST when the market officially shuts, and then opens at a different price during after-hours or pre-hours trading. The buying and selling that takes place during the period when the market is officially closed results in a gap in the market. When the market reopens at 9:30 a.m. EST, it climbs or drops to the new price that has been established when the market was closed during that time.

There are four types of Price Gaps that occurs in the market, which are

- Breakaway Gaps

- Runaway Gaps

- Common Gaps

- Exhaustion Gap

For the sake of illustration, we've included a chart of Apple (AAPL). When the market closed, the stock price was $174.36, and then there was news regarding the company's results, which were higher than expected. The stock price subsequently rose to $175.3 6. As a result, during after-hours trading, investors purchased more shares as a demonstration of their trust in the company, bringing the price of the stock past $188. As a result, at the next opening, AAPL was trading at the new $188, resulting in a Gap increase.

You could predict the direction of the stock's movement in the following days and months based on the price gap. A significant price differential implies that large institutions are buying in large quantities, and it is possible that this will be the case for some time.

Let's take a look at the prices of two old titans, Amazon and Apple, back in 2007, and the type of run they had after debuting at a significant discount to the market at the time.

Let's start with Amazon; in April 2007, the company's stock price increased by more than 100 percent, resulting in repeated gaps in trading. Within three months of starting at $42, the price continued to rise, eventually reaching $89. Take note of the enormous volume injection that occurred on the second gap day, which indicates that institutional investors are participating in the purchase of Amazon stock. We're talking about mutual funds, hedge funds, endowments, and a variety of other financial instruments at roughly the same moment.

Apple (AAPL) also experienced a gap to the upside in April 2017, which led to a successful break out of a base and later followed up with a 40% increase within the quarter.

In general, gaps occur in a variety of shapes and sizes and can be used to predict the direction in which a price will move over the following few days, and even weeks, ahead. Although the story is the same with all gaps, more research and practice

need be done in order to become proficient at spotting and trading gaps. Most essential, when you keep trades open overnight, make sure to safeguard your cash against big losses. Maintain the notion of employing a stop-loss order throughout the trading process. Triangles (Wedges) Wedges are, for the most part, a continuation of an already established design pattern. Bull and bear flags are a subclass of the types of wedges. They can, on sometimes, act as reversal patterns, however this is not always the case. A symmetrical triangular (wedge) pattern in a downtrend is shown here, followed by an ascending channel, which indicates the continuation of a bearish pattern.

1. From the GOOG (Google) chart above, you can see the symmetrical triangle formed at the chart's top. Recall what we said about a symmetrical triangle about an in-

dication of a breakout either way; in this case, it was a bearish breakout.

2. GOOG formed the bottom of the symmetrical triangle. This is where the bears injected more volume to overpower the bulls to end the indecision. This would have been a great point of entry if you had spotted earlier that the price would fall as you can see from the trend that followed that Google stock fell from $675 down to $450, which is a 33% drop within two months.

3. At this point, the stock price formed an ascending channel or a bear flag. The flag occurred while the stock was already in a bearish trend, forming a small upward sloping channel to the upside.

4. At this stage, the attempts to reverse the trend could not hold water, so the trend continued and further broke support to make new lows. You could have entered another sell order at point 4 if you spotted it.

Head and Shoulders

Inversion patterns, such as heads and shoulders, are one of the most well-documented types of patterns. It occurs when a stock in a bullish trend hits a resistance level, then pulls back a little, then breaks the resistance level a little before reversing to begin a negative trend started by a sell-off, and eventually falls through the "neckline" to a new all-time low point. The pricing action and all of the movement culminate in the formation of what appears to be two shoulders with a head in the middle.

The traditional head and shoulder pattern is the same as the inverse head and shoulder pattern, with the exception that in the case of inverse patterns, the formation is upside down instead of the typical way. Additionally, they are infrequent, but when they do occur, they are extremely powerful and signal a significant shift in the price of a stock's momentum.

The graphic below depicts not only a head and shoulders pattern, but also a wedge pattern, among other things.

Bull and Bear Traps

It happens to every trader at some point: they come across a position that appears promising, especially after they have done everything they can to prepare for that entry, but after plunging in, they find they are caught. What occurs in a bear trap is exactly what you would expect. Whenever you anticipate a bullish breakout, all of your projections swing around and head in the other direction within a short period of time after entering the market. What occurred there is that you were caught in a bull trap, and you didn't even know it.

The market is frequently plagued with bull and bear traps, and there aren't many traders who haven't been trapped in one or both at some point in their trading lives. Traps are thought to be dangerous because of the following reasons:

- Algorithmic traders and hedge funds see the price points where most automatic stop buy orders are waiting to be triggered. They know where most buyers are and wait to jump in to push the volume further up.

- The next thing they do is to buy enough stocks that will trigger most of the buy orders.

- Then follow by selling large volumes into the strength to take profits, and potentially net short later on. So, the investors who bought into what they thought was a breakout are subsequently trapped with a losing position by the reversal that just occurred.

These are disappointing situations for traders because when you think your strategy is locked down, something goes wrong, and you fall into the trap. Here are some examples to give you a better picture of what we are talking about.

To avoid or lessen the effects of traps, one of the most effective strategies is to utilize correct position sizing and to apply stop-losses to

all of

your trades. You could want to explore purchasing, say, 50% of the shares with your first order

at the moment

of the first breakout, and then adding another 50% over the course of a second purchase to make up the difference.

In the event that

you are like me and prefer to play it safe, go with 25 percent each. This way, as the price moves to confirm the real break out, you can increase your position, and if it turns out to be a trap, your loss will not be as severe as it would be if you had gone in 100% and with multiple entries.

Stock Charts Tell Stories

When it comes to stock trading, one of the benefits of using technical analysis is that the more you practice, the more you will learn about the stock and its history, which will help you make better decisions. In the following example, Dry Bulk Shipper DryShips (DRYS) had a rally of more than 1200 percent from the middle of 2007 to the beginning of 2008, reaching a high of $131.48 in October 2008. The stock then began to decline from there, plummeting by 96 percent before returning to a single-digit price level. It is possible to predict the stock's future in both the short and long term by employing technical analysis and indicator-based trading.

The years 2006 and 2007 were really good for commodities because they were extremely hot at the time and everyone who was an investor had some kind of position in them. Keeping in mind what they say about any party, they all must come to an end, the same was true for commodities.

To illustrate these concepts, we will use the DRYS chart as a starting point. Below are five critical concepts to learn about technical analysis and how to exploit trends.

1. Trends are solid and robust. Check out the run from a little under $10 in mid-2007 to $131 in October 2008. That is 1200% plus. No company experiences such a run by acci-

dent. What happened was that institutions were acquiring shares of DRYS in bulk as commodities continued to soar.

Never fight a trend; instead, join a trend at a good point and enjoy the ride.

2. Some technical patterns are prone to failure. For example, the "W" shaped pattern was considered a faulty base because the 2nd dip was not lower than the first. Patience is required in this type of situation to allow the stock to shake off any uneasy holders before the uptrend picks up, but in this case, it never picks up. Remember what we said about a trap earlier? This is one of them.

3. Heavy distribution or accumulation identifies new trends. The weeks where DRYS experienced heavy distribution were between May and June 2008 and the central turning point for the stock. It was the beginning of a reversal in DRYS' more than one-year rally.

4. Consolidation often signals the sign of a big move which could be a continuation or a reversal. For example, for nearly two months, DRYS and companies in similar situations like GNK and EXM were trading in a tight range, such that the moment the price dropped below the range, investors lost confidence and commenced selling. When there's a price consolidation, the breakout can be either a bearish or bullish one.

5. Know when to walk away. Sometimes, this might be the only strategy you need to apply to some trades as a trader. For example, any trader who entered the DRYS bullish rally later and later got caught up in the reversal thinking it would come back up would have been trapped for a long time because the

price never went up. It was a bearish rally from the moment the reversal kicked into place. When you find yourself in a losing position, you either stop-loss or cut your losses and move on.

Here's another example: this time, the chart shows Travelzoo's (TZOO) stock fall. The stock rallied from $20 to $103.80 within the space of eight months. Then came the reversal, which happened within five months, and it wiped off every previous gain and returned to $20 levels.

1. Travelzoo (TZOO) took off after a series of impressive earning releases. The main driver of the stock strengthened some institutional investors to hold on to their stock, which later fueled the bullish rally in the next few months.

2. The formation of a mini inverse head and shoulder breakout led to a bullish parabolic move. Check out the movement in December, how the price reached new lows. This is the type of trap that shakes off weak investors to trigger their stop losses prematurely.

3. The climax comes as the stock gaps on record volume (up to that point) to fresh 52-week highs. Massive gaps like this one are often marked as **exhaustion gaps** as they very typically come right before or at the top of parabolic moves. Note,

however, there are many other common topping formations; this is just one example.

4. The stock breached a two and half month consolidation in expectation of strong earnings, but immediately after the report was released, it fell to a bearish downside on record volume and began the story of the end for TZOO.

5. As the bears took over and drove the price down, you can see new lower lows forming and making the old support new resistance. And just like when a high-speed train breaks down, the rise might be quick, but the fall back to down is always quicker because it is about the loss of confidence by the investor.

Chapter Six

Chapter 6

Order Types

Perfecting the Order Types - Stop-Limit Orders

L earning and understanding how to effectively use stop-limits as a trader will help you achieve your goal and stay in the market for a longer period of time. A stop-limit order allows you to have more control over your order. You must be aware of the different forms of orders available and why you should use them, as well as the conditions that affect the execution of which order type you should employ at any given time and whether they are appropriate for your objectives.

Stop-limit Order

A stop-limit order is triggered when the stock price reaches or breaks through the submitted limit order of the specified stop price. A stop-limit is made up of two prices;

-

The stop price, which is the price that activates the order and is based on the last traded price.

- The limit price is the price constraint needed to execute the order once it is triggered.

There are no guarantees that the stop-limit order will result in an execution when it is triggered, just as there are no guarantees with limit orders. This is something you should keep in mind. A stop-limit order does not guarantee that a trade will be executed.

When to Use Stop-limit Orders

After submitting your stop-limit order, it goes to the exchange where it is placed on the order book, where it will stay until it is triggered, cancelled, or expires. Stop-limits order can only be triggered when the stock market is in session, which is between 9:30 AM to 4:00 PM EST. No trigger is expected during the pre-market and after-hour times or even when the stock is not in trading, like during bank holidays, stock halts, and weekends.

A stop-limit order can be placed for the duration of the current market session or for the duration of future market sessions. They are referred to as day orders because, if not activated, and the day was selected then stop-limit orders will expire at the end of the trading session on the day in which they were not activated. Stop-limit orders that are good-till-cancelled, on the other hand, will continue to exist and carry over to future sessions if they are not activated during the current session. Some platforms allow you to keep your order for up to 60 calendar days if it is not cancelled by the platform.

Benefits of Using Stop-limit Orders

The most significant advantage of using a stop-limit order is that it allows you to keep a close eye on your portfolio. The stop features can assist you in staying on top of the market and ensuring that you don't miss out on anything, especially when the stock prices reach your desired level of performance. In the case of a pattern that was discovered when developing your strategy, you may utilize this information to create a trigger or a stop to take advantage of a profitable chance.

Buy Stop-limit

A buy stop-limit order might assist you keep control of the price you'll pay for a certain stock you want to acquire. You can set it up and forget it once you've confirmed the maximum price per share you're willing to pay each share. The platform will place a buy order if the price rises to your chosen price or within the top price.

There are two prices involved in a stop-limit order;

1. The Stop Price: This activates the limit order to buy.

2. The Limit Price: This is the highest price you are willing to pay for each share.

With a buy stop-limit order, you direct the market to purchase shares if the price touches or goes beyond your stop price, but only if you can afford to pay a specific dollar amount or less per share.

Sell Stop-limit

A sell stop limit is an instruction to sell your stock if the price drops to or falls through the stop price. There are two prices involved in a sell stop-limit;

1. The Stop Price, which activates the limit order to sell

2. Limit Price, which decides the least price you are willing to accept from a buyer

The sell stop-limit order you place instructs the platform to execute a sale of your shares when the price drops to or below your stop price; however, you can only sell if the price drops by a certain amount of dollars or more per share, as there is a chance that the limit order will not be executed. The use of a stop-limit order is not considered to be a successful method of risk management on the bearish side by traders.

If you want to enter a sell stop-limit order that will be effective, make sure that both the stop and limit values are lower than the current bid price. Anything other than that will result in the order being activated and running as an active order.

Risks Associated with Stop-limit Order

There are various advantages to using a stop-limit order, but you must be aware that you are giving up control in return. Understanding the elements that influence how a stop-limit order is executed can assist you in deciding which risk you wish to take.

No Execution

While a stop-limit order allows you to enter a trade at a certain price or a better price, there are no guarantees that the order will be executed because the market may never reach your set point or the implied price. We've noticed multiple situations where it appears that prices were supposed to be triggered but were just a few pennies short.

Even if market movements appear to bring the price up to the limit order for a brief period, execution may be delayed if orders placed before yours take up all or part of the shares available at the current price.

Partial fills

A "partial fill," or a circumstance in which parts of the shares in your order are executed but others are not, leaves you with unfilled shares open orders, is another risk. This occurs because certain brokerage firms levy a fee after your trade is completed. You may need to consider commission costs into your orders, especially Good-Til-Closed (GTC) orders, depending on your broker and the size of the commission.

"Because all of the fills occur on the same day, multiple fills on a single order inside a single trading day only result in one commission." However, if parts of a same transaction are executed over several days, a commission may be charged for each trading day in which an execution occurs. You may be compelled to pay four different commissions if an order executes across four days." Schwab.com was used as a source.

However, by inserting precise conditions in your limit order, you can lessen the possibility of incomplete executions. "All or none," "fill or kill," "immediate or cancel," and "minimum quantity" are among the phrases you use. All of these are unique circumstances that you might incorporate into your trading approach. You should also keep in mind that these criteria could be the reason why your transaction isn't triggered, so you'll need to know how to deal with that as well. If, and when, the stock price hits a certain level, a stop-limit order is intended to be automatically triggered. If your plan ensures the price, this might be a very useful tool. At the same time, it's critical to comprehend the danger and figure out how to effectively employ this order type to improve your trade and profits.

Perfecting the Order Types - Limit Order

A limit order, like a stop-limit order, allows the trader to have greater control over the execution of their order. When it comes to matching order types to your trading strategy and goals, understanding the types of orders, why and when you can use them, as well as the elements that lead to the execution, can be extremely beneficial.

A limit order is an instruction to purchase a certain stock at a predetermined maximum price per share or to sell a specific stock at a predetermined minimum price per share at a predetermined maximum price per share. If you're placing a buy limit order, you're effectively asking the trading platform to purchase a specific stock on your behalf at the greatest price you're ready to pay for each piece of stock. In contrast, when you place a sell limit order, you are instructing the trading platform to sell a certain stock on your behalf at the lowest price possible, which is the amount of money you are ready to part with for each share of stock.

We have included a list of conditions that must be met before the order will become effective, which you should review carefully. Although a limit order allows you greater control over the price of execution, there is no guarantee that your order will be executed quickly or at all during the specified time period.

When to Use Limit Orders

In contrast to a market order, which can only be executed while the market is open, a limit order can be filed for execution throughout the pre-market, standard, and after-hours trading sessions, allowing for greater flexibility. The most noticeable distinction is that limit orders for both pre-market and after-hours trading can only be executed during electronic trading sessions, which are from 7:00 a.m. to 9:25 a.m. ET for pre-market trading and 4:05 p.m. to 8:00 p.m. ET for after-hours trading. Furthermore, if they have not been triggered or executed by the end of the trading session, they will expire at the end of the trading session. Orders placed on a day limit always expire at the end of the trading session for that day. They will not be carried over to the after-hours sessions unless they are specifically requested.

Always proceed with caution during the pre-market and after-hours trading sessions, primarily because the liquidity available is small compared to what is available during a typical market session.

Benefits of Using Limit Order

Here are some of the reasons and benefits of using limit orders.

Price Ceilings/Price Floors

Trading in a fast-moving or volatile market requires the ability to set a ceiling buy price and a floor sale price, which becomes extremely vital to your trading strategy. The use of limit orders during these times allows you to receive exactly what you want at the exact price that is suitable for your needs and budgets.

Pre-market and After-hours Sessions

While market orders are ineffective during the pre-market and after-hours trading sessions, you can use a limit order to participate in these prolonged trading sessions if you like. Aside from that, you can choose whether or not you wish to carry over the limit orders you placed during regular trading hours to a subsequent trading session. Some platforms allow you to save your data for up to 6 calendar days.

Risk Associated with Limit Order

The benefits that limit orders offer traders are great, but what are the tradeoffs? It's essential to understand the condition that can influence how a limit order will execute or whether it will execute at all.

No Execution

You may recall that we previously stated that a limit order allows you to select a better price to buy or sell at? It is important to understand that placing a limit order does not guarantee that the order will be triggered or executed because the stock's price may never reach the price you choose.

Even if it appears that trading activity is getting close to your set limit order, there is no certainty that your order will be executed because the orders placed before of yours may have used up all of the shares available at the current market price. Furthermore, when comparing market orders to limit orders, market orders always take precedence in terms of execution.

A common practice among skilled traders is to position their limit orders slightly above the asking price for buy limit orders and slightly below the asking price for sell limit orders in order to avoid these types of situations from occurring. With these, there is limited room for price volatility while still providing protection against unanticipated price triggers.

Partial Fills

There's also the possibility of "partial fills," which execute portion of the shares in an order while leaving the rest as open orders. Several brokerage firms provide a commission-free trading platform, while others charge a commission on each deal. Multiple fills on a single order during a single trading day result in a single commission being charged for all fills on that day. When your orders are fulfilled in stages over several days, you will be charged various commissions for each day they are completed. For example, if all of your limit orders take five days to execute, you will be charged commission for each of those five days.

Applying conditions to your limit orders is one way to lessen the risk of partial execution. Specifics such as "all or none," "fill or kill," "immediate or cancel," and "minimum quantity" might be included. They can assist you in fine-tuning your limit orders. However, you should be aware that these circumstances could potentially prevent your limit order from being executed.

Limit orders are useful trading tools if your strategy calls for buying and selling at certain prices and you're willing to bear the risk of the order not being executed at all.

Perfecting the Order Types - Market Order

Knowing what a market order is, how to use it, and when to use it provides you more control over your trade. What variables influence the placement of a market order and the decision to place one? These are some of the details you should consider before placing a market order.

The most frequent of all the order types available in stock trading is a market order. It's an instantaneous command to purchase or sell at the next available ask price. Keep in mind that the next trade price has no bearing on the execution of your market order.

The fill price of a market order is determined by the next available bid or ask when the order reaches its execution turn. In most cases, a market order is expected to be executed immediately; however, this does not guarantee that you will receive the stock at the specified price.

When to Use Market Orders

Market orders are day orders, which means they are only valid for the standard stock market trading session, which starts by 9:30 AM EST and closes by 4:30 PM EST. market orders cannot be used to execute orders during pre-market after-hours sessions. All orders placed outside the standard market session will only come into effect when the market opens.

Benefits of Using Market Order

The key benefit of a market order is that it is the best option when you want to enter a deal right away. They're best employed when the pricing is right for you to get in right away and you're certain you want to fill in the blanks, or when you need something done straight immediately. In this case, you're not relying on the platform to carry out your pre-programmed command; instead, you're assuming command and carrying it out yourself.

However, the desire to enter or exit a transaction using a market order should take precedence over the desire to control the price, because you will have no influence over the price and the likely commission that would follow. When there is a lot of volatility in a stock, some brokers will raise the commission charged on it.

Only use market orders if your strategy reveals that the desire to control the execution price surpasses the requirement to enter a deal.

Risk Associated with Market Order

Some factors affect the execution of market orders that traders need to be aware of, so you can factor them into your strategy.

Market Closure

When it comes to market order execution, timing is crucial. Market orders submitted outside of regular trading hours, such as pre-market or after-hours, will not be considered for execution until the market opens. Entering a market order outside of the market session is extremely riskier because you never know how it will open. After all, the pre-market and after-hours momentum cannot be compared to the active market session's.

Between sessions, a lot happens, and the order will be executed at the bid or ask price, which may or may not be what you expected. Many times, the market begins with a gap, resulting in a negative execution of your order. You then hustle to figure out how to exit the trade, and if you're not careful, your plan for the day or week will be fouled up. As a result, numerous brokers refuse to accept market orders during extended trading hours.

Fast Markets

Another risk that prevents market order execution at your preferred price is market speed, especially during periods of extreme volatility. When the market swings, especially when volume is strong, the price you expect to get may not be the price you get when your execution is finally done.

Unexpected or negative execution is always a possibility with market orders. Furthermore, due to the quickness with which market orders are processed, it is frequently hard to cancel an order once it has been filed. This is due to the fact that the platform and brokers are dealing with hundreds of requests similar to yours at the same time, thus you must be in a queue. However, you can help yourself by double-checking your order before submitting it for execution, as you are unlikely to be able to change it before it is executed.

Liquidity

When you place an order at the market price, which is the current bid or ask price, you'll probably get different prices for different parts of the transaction, especially if the stock has a lot of orders compared to the available liquidity. Consider the stock's liquidity while deciding on the type of order you want to place, such as a market order.

Due to lower participation, the impact of liquidity is felt more when trading stocks with low volume. It's likely that there may be a small number of outstanding shares or that the trading volume would be low. Because trades may have occurred within the minute or hours, the trading price you see may not be the current price you observe. In other words, the fewer shares moved, the higher the potential influence of each transaction on the next available bid or ask price.

When shares are not available to purchase or sell at the present price, individual transactions can wipe out the bid or ask. In another case, this scenario arises when a market order, usually for a large number of shares, exceeds the number of shares available at the best bid or ask. The subsequent fill pricing may differ from the original fill price.

No Market for the Stock

When there is no bid or ask for a market order, it is usually not executed. Your order will not complete if you intend to acquire 200 shares of a stock but there are no offers for that quantity to sell. Similarly, if you placed a market order to sell your shares but no bids to buy them were placed, the sell order would not be filled.

A market order will not execute if the stock in question is not accessible for trading, which could be due to late trading, a pause on the stock, or the stock is no longer available to be traded, as with other forms of orders.

Market orders are an excellent way to ensure that your strategy is executed quickly. You are aware of and willing to accept the risk of unexpected and adverse execution, particularly in terms of price volatility. You should be aware of the impact of market hours, liquidity, and market speed on your market orders as a trader.

Chapter Seven

Chapter 7

Moving Averages

A moving average is a technical indicator that smooths out price data to create a trend tracking indicator. The MA does not predict the price of stocks on its own; rather, it defines the price direction. Because it relies on prior prices to identify trend direction, the MA is a lagging indicator.

Although it does not determine price movement, it does assist in smoothing it and filtering out noise. The Bollinger Bands, McClellan Oscillator, and MACD are all technical indicators that use Moving Averages as a foundation. The Simple Moving Average (SMA) and the Exponential Moving Average (EMA) are the most well-known and widely utilized MAs (EMA). Both MAs can be used to determine the direction of a trend and to establish support and resistance levels.

The price data is smoothed over a given time range, such as daily, ten days, five hours, weekly, or any other time window you choose. Moving averages are excellent technical tools for both long and short-term trades, known for its ability to be built on a variety of time frames and to employ different numbers of the day for averaging intervals. When the price of a stock passes over the MA, it can generate a trading signal for you to use as a technical signal.

Benefits of Using Moving Averages

A moving average can aid in the clarity of your trading strategy by filtering out the "noise" that can be found on a price chart. By observing the direction of the moving average, you may obtain a rapid sense of which direction the price is moving in the short term. Whenever the moving average thread is curved up and under the candlesticks, it might be seen as an overall bullish trend. Alternatively, if the MA thread is angled downward, then indicates that the general trend is bearish. A price range is shown by a sideways thread, which indicates that the price is in a range.

There are times when the moving average can also act as a support and resistance level for the market. In the chart below, a 50-day, 100-day, or 200-day moving average (MA) can act as a support level. When the price reaches or gets close to the average, it acts like a floor, causing the price to rise. In a negative trend, the moving average functions as a resistance, similar to a ceiling, that the price must overcome before it can begin to decline once more.

Price movement may or may not adhere to the floor and ceiling theories depending on the level of volatility in the market at any given time. Frequently, the price will go through the points, pause, and then reverse  before hitting any of them. Support and resistance will be discussed in greater depth later in this chapter. However, a basic rule of thumb will be that when the price is above the moving average thread, you are looking at a positive trend in the market. The opposite is true: when the price of a stock falls below the MA thread, the stock is in a negative trend. Occasionally, MAs with different lengths can be found; in these instances, one thread will indicate a bullish trend while the other will indicate a bearish trend. We will go through this in further detail later.

Types of Moving Averages

There are different methods of calculating moving averages, but we will be focusing on the Simple Moving Average (SMA) and the Exponential Moving Average (EMA).

Calculating Simple Moving Average (SMA)

In order to calculate the simple moving average you see on the chart, you must calculate the average price of a stock over a predetermined number of periods. Remember that this indicates that the moving average is a trailing instrument, as most moving averages are constructed based on closing prices. For example, a 5-day simple moving average (SMA) is the average of the closing prices of a stock over the previous five days divided by five. All of the averages are connected to one another, which results in a single flow line. As the name implies, the moving average travels up and down (changes). When an old piece of data is deleted, a new piece of data becomes immediately available, causing the average to shift along the time scale. For the purposes of this example, you are looking at a 5-day moving average that has been evolving over the course of three days.

Daily Closing Prices: 11,12,13,14,175,16,17

Day 1 of the 5-day SMA: $(11 + 12 + 13 + 14 + 15) / 5 = 13$

Day 2 of the 5-day SMA: $(12 + 13 + 14 + 15 + 16) / 5 = 14$

Day 3 of the 5-day SMA: $(13 + 14 + 15 + 16 + 17) / 5 = 15$

Here's a breakdown of what you're looking at:

Keep in mind that we are looking at a 5-day SMA. Consequently, on Day 1, the SMA covers the previous five days, and on Day 2, the indicator drops the first date (11) because a new one has been available on Day 1. In the following day, the new data (16) is added to the Day 2 SMA to arrive at 14, and by Day 3, a new data (17) becomes accessible again.

Consequently, 16 is no longer in play, and 17 comes into play to give you 15 as the new price. This is a straightforward example in which the price steadily went from 11 to 17 over the course of seven days, and the moving average similarly increased from 13 to 15 during the course of three days of calculation. You will also observe that each MA value is a fraction of a percent lower than the previous price. For example, the moving average of Day 1 is equal to 13, but the most recent price is equivalent to 15. Prices had been lower for four days before to that, causing the moving average to lag.

Calculating Exponential Moving Average (EMA)

The key characteristic of the exponential moving average is that it eliminates the lag by giving greater weight to recent values. The weight given to the most recent price is determined by the number of periods in the moving average. An exponential Moving Average differs from a simple moving average in that the EMA calculation for a given day is dependent on the EMA calculation for all of the days before that day. In order to arrive at an acceptable or accurate 10-day EMA, you must have data over a period of time that is longer than the ten days involved.

There are three steps involved in the calculation of EMA.

Step 1: Calculate the SMA for the first EMA. Since the calculation of an EMA has to start somewhere, the best place to start is the SMA of the previous periods.

Step 2: Calculate the weighted multiplier.

Step 3: Calculate the EMA for each day between the original EMA value and the current day using the price, the multiplier, and the EMA for the previous period's value.

Here's an example of a 10-day Exponential Moving Average:

Initial SMA: the sum of 10-period / 10

Multipliers: (2 / (Time Periods + 1)) = (2 / (10 + 1)) = 0. 1.1818 (18.18%).

The best part about calculating the SMA and EMA is that the platform takes care of everything for you because the indicator calculates it by default. You can also arrange it to operate during a specific time period. For example, you can plot a 50-day simple moving average (SMA) and a 50-day exponential moving average (EMA) on a single chart. You can see from the chart that the EMA reacts to price changes more quickly than the SMA, which is due to the greater weighing placed on recent price data.

This is an intriguing thing to consider: one Moving Average is not necessarily superior to the other. As a result, you cannot generalize that SMA is superior to EMA or vice versa because it is dependent on  the time span you are working with. Depending on the period you are utilizing, the SMA may perform better for a stock or other securities, and at other times, the EMA may perform better for the same stock or other securities. The period you choose for a moving average will have a significant impact on its efficacy, regardless of the sort of moving average you use.

Moving Average Length

The most commonly used moving average lengths are 10, 20, 50, 100, and 200 days, but there are others. Using these intervals, you may apply them to whatever chart and time period that you choose to work with. You can apply them to minute charts, hour charts, daily charts, weekly charts, or even monthly charts. Your moving average's effectiveness will be determined by the length of the "look back period" you choose to apply it to. The length of your "look back period" will affect the effectiveness of your moving average. In some cases, your MA will react more quickly when you are looking back at a shorter time span. In other cases, your MA will respond more slowly when you are looking back at a longer time span.

Stock traders that focus their analytical tactics on short-term time frames can benefit from employing the 20-day moving average since the price follows the trend line much more closely, minimizing the lag period compared to 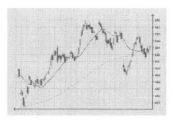 when using a longer-term moving average. The 100-day moving average can be more advantageous for traders who are looking to trade for the long term.

The amount of time it takes for the moving average indicator to suggest a potential trend reversal is known as lag. Take a look back at what we discussed previously regarding the general criteria for using moving averages. A bullish trend is defined as a price that is higher than the moving average thread, and a bearish trend is defined as a price that is lower than the moving average thread. When the price falls below its moving average, it indicates that a trend change is likely to occur in the near future, as shown by the moving average. A 20-day moving average will provide a more rapid signal for a trend reversal than a 100-day moving average in most cases. A moving average can be as short as 1, as long as 100, as long as 200, and more. When looking at historical prices, you can change the moving average to get more accurate indications.

Trading Crossovers

Crossovers are one of the most known moving average trading strategies. The first is a price crossover, which occurs when the price crosses above or below the moving average, signalling an impending change in trend.

Another method is to use a moving average that is both longer and shorter in duration on a single chart. It is a buy entry when the shorter-term moving average crosses above the longer-term moving average, as this signifies  that the trend is shifting to a positive tone. This form of crossing is referred to as a "golden cross" in some circles.

When the shorter-term moving average crosses below the longer-term moving average, it suggests a reversal from a bullish trend to a bearish trend and a buy signal, respectively. This cross is also referred to as a dead/death cross.

Also available is the triple crossover approach, which makes use of three moving averages. A triple crossing might have moving averages of five, ten, and twenty days, for example. When the shortest-term moving average crosses over the other two longer-term moving averages, signal is generated.

Home Depot (HD) is depicted in the chart above with a 10-day exponential moving average (green dotted line) and a 50-day moving average (red line), and the black line represents the daily closing price. Using the crossover technique, you  would have fallen for three whipsaws (false reversals) before finally getting into a successful trade, which is what happened. The 10-day exponential moving average (EMA) initially fell below the 50-day EMA toward the end of October, as indicated by the point 1 noted on the chart. Although temporary, the 10-day exponential moving average (EMA) returned to the upside in mid-November, as seen by point 2 on the chart. However, in January, at point 3 on the chart, the second bearish crossover occurred close to the November price levels, resulting in yet another whipsaw in the market's performance. The bearish cross did not stay long, as the 10-day exponential moving average (EMA) moved back above the 50-day EMA within a few days of being formed. This may be seen at the fourth point on the chart. Finally, after three false signals, the fourth one was the one that produced the best results, resulting in a 20 percent increase in the price of the company's stock.

We can take away two points from here.

Crossovers, for starters, can cause false signals or whipsaws. To avoid slipping into the whipsaws, you can use a price or time filter. If you're looking at a daily chart, you might want to wait three days or for the 10-day EMA to move above or below the 50-day EMA by a certain amount before trading the reversal.

Secondly, you can use MACD to quantify these crossovers. MACD with setting 10, 50, and 1 will give you a line representing the difference between the two EMAs. When there's a golden cross, the MACD turns positive and negative during a death cross.

You can also use the Percentage Price Oscillator (PPO) to see the percentage differences. Take note that the MACD and the PPO are based on EMA and will not match the SMA.

Oracle (ORCL) is seen in the chart above with a 50-day EMA, 200-day EMA, and MACD (50,200,1). Over the course of two and a half years, there have been four MA crossovers. The first three ended in whipsaws, which may have resulted in losses if you had  acted on them. The fourth crossover resulted in a prolonged turn-around, with Oracle's stock rising to the mid-twenties.

When the trend is strong, moving average crossovers work well, but when the trend is weak, especially in a range market, you may be fooled by false reversal signals.

Support and Resistance

As mentioned earlier, moving averages can also serve as a support in a bullish trend and resistance in a bearish trend. For example, a short-term bullish trend can find support near a 20-day SMA, also found when using Bollinger Bands. A long-term bullish trend can find support around the 200-day SMA price, which is the most common long-term MA. In fact, the 200-day MA may be the perfect support or resistance because many traders use it. It's like a prophecy come through.

From mid-2004 to the end of 2008, this graph illustrates the NY Composite with the 200-day SMA. During the bullish trend, the 200-day SMA acted as support numerous times, and when the trend reversed with a double top support break, the 200-day functioned as support around 9,500 levels.

It is incorrect to assume support and resistance levels from moving averages all of the time, especially the longer MAs. Emotions often drive the market, resulting in overshooting. Use the MAs to identify support and resistance levels rather than expecting the exact level.

Identifying Trends Using MAs

Regardless of whether you're using a simple moving average or an exponential moving average, the direction offers you with a wealth of information. A rising MA, for example, implies a general increase in the price of that stock, whereas a falling MA signals continuous selling and a decrease in price. A long-term moving average that is rising implies a long-term bullish trend, whereas one that is falling shows a long-term bearish trend.

In the chart above, you can see 3M (MMM) with a 150-day exponential moving average (EMA). When the trend is strong, the effectiveness of the MA is demonstrated in this figure. In November 2007

and again in January 2008, the 150-day exponential moving average (EMA) became negative. Take note of how it dipped by 15% before reversing direction and moving in the direction of the MA. Another characteristic of trailing indicators is that they detect trend reversals either as they occur (at the very best) or after they have taken place (at worst). 3M continued to decline until March 2009, when it had a 40-50 percent increase. One more lag to be aware of: the EMA did not turn bullish until after the spike, but once it did, the bullish trend continued for another 12 months. When the trend is clear and robust, moving averages (MAs) perform flawlessly.

The Lag Factor

During our discussion of moving averages, we have made numerous references to the "lag." Let's have a look at what it implies in this context with an example.

The greater the length of a moving average, the greater the lag. A 10-day exponential moving average (EMA) will hug prices closely and turn slightly after the prices have turned. Short MAs are similar to motorcycles in that they are maneuverable and quick to turn. A 100-day moving average, on the other hand, will take longer to react than a 10-day moving average because it has more historical data. The lengthier MAs are large ships that are sluggish and difficult to turn.

To shift a 100-day moving average, a greater and more sustained price movement is required.

Moving Average Ribbons

You have several MAs with different look-back periods on a single chart. The moving average is like a ribbon as it moves across the chart.

While evaluating the individual information that the moving average lines on the ribbon provide you with, you can also gain additional information by looking at the ribbon it-

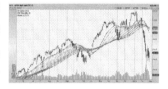

self. For example, when the lines are running parallel, it signals a strong trend that is now in force, and when the ribbon begins to spread (the lines begin to move apart), it shows that the trend is weakening and eventually terminating. If the lines begin to contract, move closer together, or even cross, this indicates a reversal of the current trend.

Downsides of Moving Averages

Calculated using historical data, moving averages are a type of trend line. Nothing in the setup or technique is a prediction or a look into the future. As a result, the outcomes of MAs are frequently unpredictable. The price movement tends to accept the moving average support and resistance levels and trade signals on certain occasions and disregards the indications on other occasions, depending on the situation. In addition, when using moving averages, the price becomes choppy, swinging back and forth and generating a large number of bogus reversals and trade signals. You should either step back and let it play out on its own or, better yet, utilize another indication to determine the trend when you notice this. The same is true for moving average crossovers when the MAs become entangled for an extended period of time, resulting in a whipsaw effect and the execution of repeated lost trades. When the trend is strong and clear, moving averages are good, but they perform poorly when the market is in a range. You might be able to come up with a temporary solution if you can adjust the time frame. It's probable that certain false signal difficulties will linger even after the adjustment has been made; therefore, you should keep an eye on the market's lead indicators to guarantee your trend is in good shape.

Lead Indicators

Lead indicators for equities are interest rates, the relative strength index, and unemployment rates.

Taking Interest Rates into Account

In today's domestic economy, interest rates are one of the most frequently debated indicators. The reason for this is rather simple. Banks and other lenders raise their interest rates for consumer lending as the Federal Reserve raises interest rates – or the cost of borrowing money. As a result, entrepreneurs and small business owners frequently hesitate before taking out big business loans.

As a result, growth rates in the domestic economy may remain stable. Reduced interest rates, on the other hand, frequently lead to increased borrowing incentives, which stimulates growth and supports the economy. This is especially useful during economic downturns or stagnation.

When it Comes to Unemployment Rates

The link between unemployment rates and stock market activity is quite obvious. With a rising unemployment rate, a larger percentage of working-age persons is being forced out of the workforce. As a result, consumer spending is anticipated to fall. It is extremely usual for corporate revenue to decline when consumer spending levels fall. With this in mind, rising unemployment rates are frequently accompanied by strong stock market selloffs. When unemployment rates decline, there is usually a rise in investment dollars in the stock market.

Investigating the Relative Strength Index (RSI)

The relative strength index, or RSI, was created by Welles Wilder and is used to describe the current momentum of the stock market. It is produced from calculations linked to recent gains or losses in the market. A time frame is created, and the number of gains and losses experienced by a particular stock are utilized as part of a wider computation to determine if the stock is currently oversold or overbought. During times of market volatility, this knowledge might be especially useful. If you're unsure whether or not it's the proper moment to buy a stock, the RSI can help you predict what the next probable market activity might be.

Chapter Eight

Chapter 8

The Keltner Channel

An additional trailing technical indicator, the Keltner Channel helps traders spot trend reversals, breakouts, and overall direction. When a trend appears to be losing momentum, these channel lines can also be used to indicate overbought and oversold levels on the chart. It is a technical indicator that is based on volatility and falls under the category of bands. You may place it both above and below an exponential moving average.

The Bollinger Bands technical indicator, which employs standard deviation to set the bands, is similar in appearance and operation to this indicator. Instead of using the standard deviation to determine channel distance, the Keltner Channels employ the Average True Range (ATR) to determine channel distance.

For the greatest results, the ATR values for the channels are normally set two ATR values above and below the 20-day exponential moving average. The EMA defines the direction, while the ATR specifies the width of the channel. As soon as the stock's price action crossed the upper Keltner Channel, the prevailing trend for that stock was determined to be bullish. When the price approaches the lower Keltner Channel, on the other hand, the trend becomes bearish. In addition, the angle of the channel can be used to determine the direction of the current trend. It is also possible to interpret the price oscillation between the upper and lower channels as a support and resistance level.

Breaking Down the Keltner Channel

The original formula Simple moving averages (SMA) and high-low prices were utilized to create the bands by Chester Keltner in the 1960s. Linda Bradford

Raschke

, on the other hand, produced a novel formula in the 1980s that is still widely used today. This time, the average true range is used (ATR).

The Keltner Channel is made up of three lines, the middle of which is an EMA of the price. The exponential moving average (EMA) levels have lines above and below them. The top band is usually placed twice the ATR above the EMA, while the lower band is usually set twice below the EMA. As volatility defined by the average true range expands and collapses, the bands respond and react accordingly.

Price action should mostly stay within the upper and lower bands, also known as the channels. As a result, price movements outside of the channels can indicate trend shifts and breakouts. Again, the channel's direction, such as up, down, or sideways, might aid in determining the trend's direction.

The Keltner Channel Calculation

There are basically three steps to calculating the Keltner Channel.

Step 1: Choose the length of the Exponential Moving average (EMA)

Step 2: Choose the time/period for the AVR

Step 3: Select the Average True Range (AVR)

Middle Line: 20-day EMA

Upper Channel Line: 20-day EMA + (2 x ATR (10))

Lower Channel Line: 20-day EMA - (2 x ATR (10))

This is the default setting for a stock chart, and it can be changed at any time. The more you practice the technique, the more likely it is that you will find a situation that is optimal for your method. Knowing that the moving average is based on historical price, it should come as no surprise that a longer moving average will have more lagged information, while a shorter moving average will have less lagged information. The volatility setting is determined by the average true range. As a result, using a short time frame, such as 10, will result in a more volatile ATR that changes as the 10-period fluctuates and flows in and out. On the other hand, longer time frames, such as 100 days, level out the swings and result in a more consistent average true range measurement.

The multiplier has the most influence on the width of the channel.... For example, merely changing the figure from 2 to 1 will reduce the channel by 50% in size. Additionally, simply raising the number of columns from 2 to 3 will expand the width by 50%.

The chart below shows three Keltner Channels with setting at 1,2 and 3 average true range away from the central MA.

You can see the default Keltner Channels in red, followed by
a wider channel in blue, and then
another narrower channel in green.
The blue channels had a set of
AVR values above and below 3x
ATR; for the green channel, we
used 1 ATR value. All three channels share the 20-day EMA, which
is represented by the dark dotted
lines in the middle of the chart.

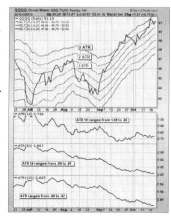

The ATR for 10, 50, and 100 periods is represented by three different
ATR values in the chart indicator window.

Take note of how the short ATR (10 periods) reacts more volatilely
as the range of the chart increases. The 100-period average real range,
on the other hand, appears to be smoother and less volatile than the
previous one.

What do these mean?

Technical indicators such as channels, envelopes, and bands are
intended to capture the majority of price movement. Because they
are unusual events, when you notice movement outside or below the
channel lines, you should pay close attention to what you are seeing.
Trends are frequently characterized by a rapid movement in one way
or the other. Rallying above the upper channel coil could be indicative
of the resurgence of bullish momentum, while a free fall below the
lower channel coil could indicate widespread selling and weakness in
the stock price. When this type of movement occurs, it might herald
the conclusion of an existing trend or it could mark the beginning of
a new trend.

With the exponential moving average (EMA) as its foundation, the Keltner Channel is a trend following indicator; that is, it is based on historical data and does not make predictions about the future. As is the case with all moving averages and other indicators in the "trend-following" category, the Keltner Channel is a lagging indicator in the market. The direction of the channel is determined by the movement of the moving average. In most cases, when the channels are facing upward and moving upward, the market is in a bullish move or an uptrend. Alternatively, when it is pointing downwards and continues to fall, you are looking at a bearish trend. When the market is trading in a range, the channel travels sideways.

Breakouts or uptrends could be signalled when the channel is on an upturn and breaks above the upper trend line; however, if the channel breaks below the lower trend line, it could signify a bearish breakout or a downtrend. You will also come across situations where the price action breaks through the upper channel, but prices bounce between the channel lines instead of breaking through them. This type of range is indicated by a flat MA. The channel's borders can then be used to determine overbought or oversold levels, at which point you can enter a sell or buy position for at least a temporary reversal.

Keltner Channels vs Bollinger Bands

Here are two key differences between Bollinger Bands and Keltner Channels that you should be aware of.

1. Because the width of the Bollinger Bands is determined by the standard deviation, which is more volatile than the ATR, the Keltner Channels are smoother than the Bollinger Bands in several ways. These channels are considered advantageous because they maintain a more consistent width, which makes

them ideal for trend spotting and following, according to industry experts.

2. The Keltner Channels are based on the exponential moving average (EMA), which is more sensitive than the simple moving average (SMA) employed in Bollinger Bands.

In the chart below, the Keltner Channel is shown in blue, Bollinger Bands are shown in pink, and ATR 10, Standard Deviation 10, and Standard Deviation 20 are shown for comparison purposes. Observe the fact that the Keltner Channels are smoother than the Bollinger Bands and that the Standard Deviation spans a wider range than the Average True Range.

Bullish or Uptrend

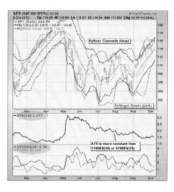

As shown in the chart below, Archer Daniels Midland (ADM) started a bullish trend when the Keltner Channels began to rise and the stock rose over the upper section of the channel line. As you can see in the chart below, ADM was in an unmistakable bearish decline from April to May, with prices tearing through the lower channel. However, a wave of strong purchasing began in June, pushing prices above the upper channel level, resulting in a positive trend that continued into the summer. You can also observe that prices were able to maintain their position above the bottom channel despite dips in late July.

Even after establishing a new uptrend, it's a good idea to wait for a
pullback to get a better entry point
and boost your reward-to-risk ratio.
You can also use a momentum oscillator to identify the overbought and
oversold levels on the chart. This will

be really beneficial in terms of a better access point. The Stochastic
RSI, which is one of the more sensitive momentum indicators in
activity, dips below in this chart. During the bullish ascent, it dips to
.20 to enter oversold levels three times. Then crosses back over . 20
which is a favorable sign that the upswing that has been in place will
resume.

Bearish or Downtrend

The following chart depicts Nvidia (NVDA) beginning a downtrend with a severe breach below the lower channel line at the top
of the chart. However, after the initial break, the stock encountered
resistance near the middle channel line, following the initial breach
of the 20-day exponential moving average, which occurred between
mid-May and early August. The inability of prices to rise closer to the
upper channel line is a strong indication of the downtrend's continuation.

The momentum oscillator's 10-period Commodity Channel Index (CCI) displays a short-term overbought condition. All price levels above the 100 level are deemed overbought on this CCI, and any fall below the 100 level will result in a continuation of the neg-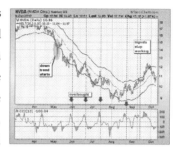

ative downward trend. The signal functioned nicely until September, as evidenced by the chart. The subsequent failed signal could have been due to a trend reversal, which was confirmed when the upper channel line was breached.

Flat or Range Trend

The Keltner Channel can also be used to identify a flat or range trend. You can utilize the Keltner channels to detect overbought and oversold price levels once the range has been identified. A trading range is a flat moving average that can be easily spotted using the Average Direc- tional Index, another technical indicator (ADX). Between February and late September, IBM fluctuated between support around the 120 - 122 levels and resistance around the 130 - 132 levels, as shown in the chart below. From April to September, the middle line, the 20-day exponential moving average, lagged but finally straightened out.

The ADX (black line) may be seen in the indicator pane, confirming the trend's weakness. The low and decreasing ADX indicates a trend that is losing strength. The ADX is high and rising, indicating signifi- cant strength. For the most part, ADX was below 40 and 30 for a long time, indicating a range rather than a trend. It's also worth noting that the ADX peaked in early June before declining till August.

If you have the potential of a weak trend and an active price range, you can use Keltner channels to look for reversals. You'll also observe how the channel lines correspond to the support and resistance levels. The price of IBM shares dropped three

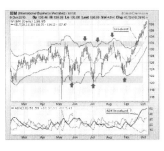

times between May and August. These are entry sites with a low risk of failure. The stock came close to reaching the top channel line before reverting at the resistance price.

In the Disney chart below, we find a similar situation:

Interpreting the Keltner Channel

The chart below is that of gold futures, and it gives a great insight into the Keltner Channel with a 20-day MA an ATR multiplier of 1.5.

Keltner Channel
Daily Chart - 100 oz Gold (ZG)

Buy when Price closes above Upper Band of Keltner Channel

Sell when Price closes below Lower Band of Keltner Channel

Buy

Keltner Channel
(20-day EMA, 1.5 x ATR)

There are numerous ways to interpret the Keltner Channel, and I must agree that some of these approaches are rather complicated; that is why you are getting this Keltner strategy segment. We'll look at how to spot breakouts, as well as oversold and overbought readings.

Price Breakouts

Possible Buy Signal – When the price closes above the upper band, buy.

Possible Sell Signal – When the price closes below the lower band, sell.

Caution: Applying other technical tools like the examples above would be safe for best buy or sell entry. This will give you leverage and room for more profit and avoid entering a trend that has run out of steam.

Overbought & Oversold Readings

The Keltner breakout strategy could also work well when there's a change from a flat or range market to a bullish or bearish trend.

Trading a range market or stock can be tricky, but the Keltner Channel makes it easier and profitable because it provides you with overbought and oversold levels along with support and resistance during a range market.

The Nasdaq 100 ETF (QQQQ) shows us a good example of a flat market in the chart below. In the chart below:

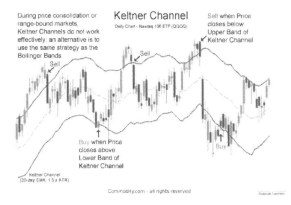

Keltner Channel
Daily Chart - Nasdaq 100 ETF (QQQQ)

During price consolidation or range-bound markets, Keltner Channels do not work effectively: an alternative is to use the same strategy as the Bollinger Bands

Sell

Sell when Price closes below Upper Band of Keltner Channel

Sell

Buy when Price closes above Lower Band of Keltner Channel

Buy

Keltner Channel (20-day EMA, 1.5 x ATR)

Potential Buy Signal at Oversold Levels

To prevent being trapped in a potential downtrend breakout, use the Keltner Channel to identify a price breakout below the lower channel. Before placing a purchase order, it's preferable to wait until the price closes back inside the channel. The difference between profiting and losing on a trade might be as little as a second's pause. A Keltner Channel outside breakout is not something you want to be caught in.

Potential Sell Signal at Overbought Levels

It's better to wait for the price to close back within the channel after a price breakthrough above the upper Keltner band. This little bit of patience could have stopped you from sliding into a bullish breakthrough trap. You would also have avoided losses and would now be in an excellent position to make a solid entry.

Bollinger Band and Keltner Channel Trading Strategy

We discussed the differences between Bollinger Bands and Keltner Channels earlier, but in this part, we'll look at more than just the similarities, focusing on a technique that combines the two indicators for the best outcome.

The Bollinger Bands and Keltner Channels are volatility channel indicators that measure and draw volatility-related lines above and below the market. Envelopes or just bands are other names for them. When stock price volatility rises, the bands widen, and when volatility falls, the bands contract or shrink, with the edges practically touching.

The Bollinger Bands and Keltner Channels are used to determine the outside limits of a price change's normalcy. It also determines where the band and channels are most likely to establish support and resistance levels, so you can prepare for something odd and plan your trading accordingly if certain levels are breached, ensuring you are in the greatest position to enter a trade or are not caught off guard.

Bounce, Walking the Bands, M-Tops, W-Bottoms, and Squeeze are some of the ways to use the Bands and Channels to generate general trading signals. In this section, we'll look at how to use the Squeeze method to spot a change in market volatility and how to make the most of your trading strategy.

Bollinger Bands

The Bollinger Bands performs different functions because they are made up of moving averages and standard deviation to detect a change in the volatility levels in the market. Below are the three components of the Bollinger Bands:

1. Upper Band: 20-SMA + (2 x Standard Deviation)

2. Middle Line: 20-period SMA

3. Lower Band: 2-SMA - (2 x Standard Deviation)

The standard deviation is a measure of the level of volatility in the market. It enables it to expand when the market's volatility is high, and to contract to the point of nearly touching when the market's volatility decreases. Several traders believe that the more price action moves towards the upper bands, the more the market moves into overbought levels, and that the more price action moves towards the lower bands, the more the market moves into oversold levels. At these levels, traders may want to consider trading pullback techniques.

Lower and Upper Bollinger band Bands

Keltner Channel

The Keltner Channel is another volatility-based technical indicator made up of three different lines, but instead of using the standard deviation as we have in Bollinger Bands, it uses the Average True Range to set channel distances.

Below are the three components of the Keltner Channel:

1. Upper Channel: 20-EMA + (2 * Average True Range)

2. Middle Line: 20-period Exponential Moving Average (EMA)

3. Lower Channel Line: 20 EMA - (2 * Average True Range)

The Keltner Channels and Bollinger Bands are similar in how they work; while Bollinger Bands uses Standard Deviation to calculate upper and lower bands, the Keltner channel uses Average True Range. The general idea is that the farther the closing price is from the average closing price, the more volatile the market is and vice versa. That is what determines the degree of expansion and contraction of the Bollinger Bands or a Keltner Channel.

Lower and Upper Keltner Channels Lines

The Squeeze Strategy

It is described as a Squeeze when the bands or channels come together, which is particularly common in a range-market. This is a period of time during which there is little action in the market or for a certain stock. For expert traders, it is a time to be on the lookout for anything that is about to happen, something that could present a trading opportunity. On the other hand, the greater the distance between the bands and channels, the more likely it is that you will be dealing with an overbought or oversold scenario, as well as decreased volatility in the near future. You should begin preparing to leave or enter a trade as earliest as possible.

A bullish or bearish breakout should be expected if the bands squeeze together, as around 90 percent of price movements occur within these boundaries. An expanding band indicates that traders are becoming more active in the market, with the expectation that the stock price will continue in the breakout direction. The greater the number of times the price breaks outside the upper band, the more likely it is that the bullish trend will continue, and the greater the number of times the price breaks outside the lower band, the more likely it is that the negative trend will continue. The goal of this technique is to catch this move when it is still in the planning stages.

The Squeeze

Setting Up the Squeeze Strategy

The squeeze approach can be used on both the Bollinger bands and the Keltner Channels, but it is more effective when used together. In general, the Keltner Channels have a tighter squeeze than the Bollinger bands do. However, the Bollinger Bands, as opposed to the Keltner Channels, are more accurate in representing market volatility since the contraction and expansion of the bands are wider and more explicit than what you would find in the Keltner Channels.

Using the two signs in conjunction, on the other hand, can help you improve the accuracy of your predictions. Both of these indicators will tend to confirm a reversal in volatility and trend, and you may utilize the Bollinger Bands breakouts as trade signals at that point. Using the default look-back duration of 20 for the two indicators in the following example, we will be capable of manipulating the upper and lower bands.

Defining the Squeeze

First and foremost, you must check that the price has stabilized and that the market volatility is low before creating buy and sell signals. There is a squeeze in place, with the top and lower bands of the Bollinger bands going inside the Keltner channel, respectively. The upper Bollinger band is a bit lower than the upper Keltner channel, and the lower Bollinger band is a little higher than the lower Keltner channel, to put it another way. Essentially, this scenario is a twofold confirmation of the squeeze, as well as an indication that the current volatility could reverse from low to high in a short period of time.

The Bullish Scenario

Having detected an established squeeze, you can be confident that a price breakout upwards that breaches the upper Bollinger Band will signal the beginning of a bullish trend in the future. As evidence for this point, consider the fact that once the price begins to breach the bands, it indicates a slowing of the squeeze and a high possibility of strong market volatility and price movement in the near future.

The Bearish Scenario

In addition, a price breakout from the lower Bollinger Bands following a squeeze indicates the probability of a bearish trend developing shortly, as well as increasing market volatility in the same direction, as investors lose trust in the stock.

How the price remained consolidated during the squeeze and plunged after a lower breakout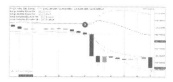

Setting Up Your Strategy

In this segment, you will see how to set up your strategy on your trading platform. For this example, we are using the "Mudrex" trading platform. Since the buy or sell signal always comes before the squeeze, then we need to apply the concept of "X Candlestick Ago." this means the Bollinger Bands should be lying inside the Keltner Channel X candles before the price breakouts. Where X = 5 is the maximum number of candlesticks that should lie between the squeeze and the breakout.

Below is our entry and exit strategy; that way, we know what to do while building our strategy.

Enter a Buy When:

- Upper Bollinger Band is less than Upper Keltner (5 Candlesticks Ago)

- Lower Bollinger Band is greater than Lower Keltner (5 Candlesticks Ago)

- The closing price is greater than Upper Bollinger.

Enter a Sell When:

- Upper Bollinger Band is less than Upper Kelter (5 Candlesticks Ago)

- Lower Bollinger Band is greater than Keltner (5 Candlesticks Ago)

- The Closing price is lower than the Lower Bollinger Band.

If the signal turns out to be a false signal, we recommend a stop loss of 10% to avoid further losses from being incurred. Stop loss orders help to increase the percentage of transactions that are profitable, which is a healthy margin. It is true that the value of your stop-loss is determined by how much risk you are willing to take on. Choosing a 10 percent stop-loss indicates that your trade will close at a loss if the deal swings against you by 10 percent in the incorrect direction during the trading session.

Compare the block for the first squeeze of a Upper Bollinger less than a Upper Keltner (5 Candlestick Ago) looks like the following.

Compare the block for the second squeeze condition of a Lower Bollinger greater than a Lower Keltner (5 Candlesticks Ago) looks like the following.

The final squeeze condition looks like the following:

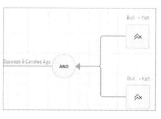

This is the same for the buy and sell signal.

We need to define the buy signal by comparing the closing price and the Upper Bolling such that the signal is triggered when the Closing Price is greater than the Upper Bollinger.

Additionally, you can set the sell signal compare block for the Closing Price less than the Lower Bollinger Band.

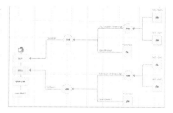

After including the 10% stop-loss, your overall squeeze strategy should look like this:

We highly recommend testing this strategy on a demo account for a few weeks before investing and trying out real money. This trial period will allow you to tweak and

make necessary adjustments and
familiarize yourself with the strategy.

Since the Bollinger Band and the
Keltner Channels notify you when
there will be a change in the market from a period of low volatility

to higher volatility, combining the two indicators should boost your
success rate better than when using just one of the two.

More Ways to Use the Keltner Channels

Keltner Channels and Bollinger
Bands are Among the Most Popular
Envelop Based Technical Indicators

Keltner Channels Can Provide
Overall Market Outlook and Generate Trading Signals

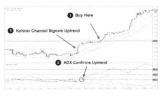

Trading Breakouts with Keltner
Channel and Average Directional
Index

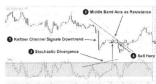

Trading Pullbacks with Keltner
Channel and Stochastic Divergence

Trading a Ranging Market with Keltner Channel, Average Directional Index, and Price Action Bars

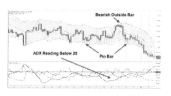

Every strategy or indicator has its drawbacks. Volatility channels have become increasingly popular and useful tools in spotting extreme short-term prices in stocks. They are designed to help you discover profitable entries for better trading successes.

Chapter Nine

Chapter 9

Standard Deviation for Stocks

R isk management is an important component of your trading plan that should be addressed properly if you want to develop and progress as a professional in the field. Risk management is crucial in economics and accounting, but it is even more vital in traders' and investors' trading and investing approaches.

If you're interested in stock trading, knowing the odds that a specific stock will move in a given direction could make the difference between making money and losing money, forcing you out of the market. Traders and financial analysts employ a variety of indicators to gauge the volatility and relative risk of potential assets, but the standard deviation is the most widely used.

The standard deviation is critical for assessing investment risk, but it is not the only instrument accessible to traders and investors. Traders can use a variety of indications to determine whether a stock is too risky for them, or even whether it is not risky enough for them. The standard deviation has been mentioned a few times in the context of detailing how specific indicators work; consequently, a quick explanation of what it is and why it is essential is in order.

We use the term standard deviation, which derives from mathematics, to describe the lack of consistency or the process of distribution around an average. This indicator also measures volatility and dispersion, with dispersion defined as the difference between actual and average values. The higher the standard deviation, the more dispersion or variability there is; the lower the standard deviation, the less dispersion or variability there is.

Standard deviation is used to estimate predicted risk and appreciate the significance of various types of price movement. Technical analysts have developed their charting abilities over the years, relying on them to assess risk, lead them away from bad investments, and forecast future trends.

Calculating

Standard Deviation

"Standard deviation is calculated by first subtracting the mean from each value, and then squaring, adding, and averaging the differences to produce the variance. While variance itself is a useful indicator of range and volatility, the squaring of the individual differences means they are no longer reported in the same unit of measurement as the original data set." Definition Extracted from Investopedia.

When it comes to stock prices, the data is in dollars, and the variation is expressed in squares of dollars, which is not primarily a unit of measure. Simply put, standard deviation is the square root of the variance, which reduces it to the original unit of measure and makes it easier to use and understand. The following are the actions to take while calculating standard deviation:

Step 1: Compute the average (mean) price for the number of periods or observations.

Step 2: Determine the deviation for each period (close less average price).

Step 3: Square each period's deviation

Step 4: Sum the squared deviations

Step 5: Divide this sum by the number of deviations

Step 6: The standard deviation equals the square root of that number (step 5).

The table above shows the standard deviation for a 10-period period, which was taken as an example from QQQQ data. Keep in mind how the 10-period average is calculated after the tenth period, and how that average is subsequently applied to all subsequent periods. Calculating a running standard deviation with this formula would take a long time.

10-period Standard Deviation of Population						
Date	QQQQ Price	10-period Average (mean)	Deviation	Deviation Squared	10-period Average of Deviation Squared	Standard Deviation
1	2-Dec-10	53.73	54.09	-0.36	0.13		
2	3-Dec-10	53.87	54.09	-0.22	0.05		
3	6-Dec-10	53.85	54.09	-0.24	0.06		
4	7-Dec-10	53.88	54.09	-0.21	0.04		
5	8-Dec-10	54.08	54.09	-0.01	0.00		
6	9-Dec-10	54.14	54.09	0.05	0.00		
7	10-Dec-10	54.50	54.09	0.41	0.18		
8	13-Dec-10	54.30	54.09	0.21	0.04		
9	14-Dec-10	54.40	54.09	0.31	0.09		
10	15-Dec-10	54.16	54.09	0.07	0.01	0.06	0.24

The standard deviation formula is easier to work with on trading platforms and spreadsheet programs like Microsoft Excel. Here's an excerpt from an Excel file that shows how to calculate standard deviation, followed by a chart to show how it works in practice.

10-period Standard Deviation of Population using STDEVP in Excel		
1-Nov-10	52.22	
2-Nov-10	52.78	
3-Nov-10	53.02	
4-Nov-10	53.67	
5-Nov-10	53.67	
8-Nov-10	53.74	
9-Nov-10	53.45	
10-Nov-10	53.72	
11-Nov-10	53.39	
12-Nov-10	52.51	(STDEVP)
15-Nov-10	52.32	0.51
16-Nov-10	51.45	0.73
17-Nov-10	51.60	0.86
18-Nov-10	52.43	0.83
19-Nov-10	52.47	0.79
22-Nov-10	52.91	0.72
23-Nov-10	52.07	0.68
24-Nov-10	53.12	0.58
26-Nov-10	52.77	0.51
29-Nov-10	52.73	0.52
30-Nov-10	52.09	0.53
1-Dec-10	53.19	0.48
2-Dec-10	53.73	0.49
3-Dec-10	53.87	0.58
6-Dec-10	53.85	0.62
7-Dec-10	53.88	0.67
8-Dec-10	54.08	0.62
9-Dec-10	54.14	0.66
10-Dec-10	54.50	0.69
13-Dec-10	54.30	0.65
14-Dec-10	54.40	0.36
15-Dec-10	54.16	0.24

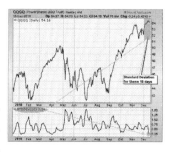

Standard Deviation Values

The stock price at the time of calculation has an impact on the standard deviation numbers. Because high prices are associated with more volatility, stocks with high prices, such as google at +550, would have a higher standard deviation than stocks with low prices, such as intel at +22. The high numbers are indicative of the stock's current market price rather than its historical price, rather than more volatility. The standard deviation figures are expressed in terms that are directly relevant to the stock's current price. Similarly, if the price of a stock swings drastically over time, historical SD values will be changed. If a stock's price rises from $10 to $50, the standard deviation (SD) at $50 will almost likely be higher than it was at $10.

The standard deviation is shown by the left-hand scale in the chart above. Google's SD scale is from 2.5 to 35, whereas Intel's scale ranges f rom.10 to.75, according to the company. When it comes to Google, the average price changes (deviations) range from $2.5 to $35, whereas the average price changes (deviations) for Intel range from $0.05 to $0.75.

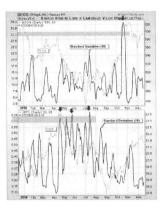

Despite the variances in range, chart specialists are able to clearly identify changes in volatility for each individual security. From April to June, Intel's volatility increased as the Standard Deviation (SD) climbed above.70 on many occasions. When the standard deviation (SD) rose above.30 in October, Google saw a spike in volatility. To directly compare the volatility of the two assets, you would need to divide the standard deviation by the closing price.

If you want to estimate the significance of a change or create expectations, you can utilize the value of the standard deviation. This is based on the assumption that price increases are regularly distributed, as depicted by the traditional bell curve. Despite the fact that price fluctuations for securities are not always normally distributed, chart experts can still apply typical distribution criteria to determine the significance of a price shift.

In a normal distribution, 68 percent of the observations fall within one standard deviation, 95 percent fall within two standard deviations, and 99.7 percent fall within three standard deviations, respectively. You should be able to estimate the significance of a price fluctuation based on the recommendations provided above. The strength or weakness of any movement greater than one standard deviation would be above average, depending on the direction of the movement.

In the Microsoft (MSFT) chart above, the indicator window shows a 21-day standard deviation. There are about 21 active trading days in a month, and the standard deviation was .88 on the last day of trading.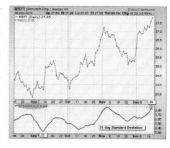

Under normal distribution, 68% of the 21 observations should show a price change of less than $0.88, while 95% of the 21 observations should show a price change of less than 1.76 (2 x .88 or two SD), and 99.7% of the observations should show a price change of less than 2.64 (3 x .88 or three SD observations). Any price movement that was 1,2 or 3 SD would be deemed noteworthy.

The 21-day SD still does not have a fixed pattern as it rises and falls between .32 and .88 from mid-August to mid-December. You can introduce a 250-day moving average that can smooth the indicator and find an average of around $0.68.

Price actions greater than $0.68 were greater than the 250-day SMA of the 21-day SD. These above-average price actions signal heightened interest that could indicate a change in trend or a breakout.

Bottom Line

The standard deviation is a mathematical measure of the degree to which something is volatile. These numbers provide the theoretical mathematician with an estimate of the price fluctuations to be predicted. Price movement that exceeds the standard deviation indicates either minor strength above average or weakness below average. The SD can also be used in conjunction with other indicators such as the Bollinger Bands. The bands can be set to be 2 standard deviations above and below a moving average, respectively. When prices move outside the bounds of the bands, it is necessary to draw attention to the situation and take action. Momentum oscillators and Keltner Channels are two further methods that can be used to support the standard deviation of a distribution.

Chapter Ten

Chapter 10

Market Strategy

There are four distinct phases that every stock runs through which could be called its lifecycle.

They are Accumulating, Advancing, Distributing and Declining. Each of these phases are in different cycles and different trading styles are needed during each of these phases. Prior to making any trade it is important to understand which phase a stock is currently residing in.

Accumulation

During the accumulation phase, the stock will often move in a range that is similar to that of the Bollinger

bands, which is sideways. One of the more advantageous trade settings is known as the Iron Corridor, and the reason for this is that it may provide gains whenever a stock is only moving in a sideways direction.

Advancing

During the advancing stage, the stock is going toward higher prices and the velocity of the stock appears to rise up during this phase as well. Purchasing stocks, utilizing call options and call spreads, and selling put options are all excellent tactics to adopt during this phase of the market.

Distributing

During the period of distribution, stock purchasers are trying to sell their shares for a profit, while others are joining in as a result of the recent action taken by the company. Lower highs and lower lows are typical of the sideways movement that characterizes the distribution phase of a market cycle. During this period of the market, butterfly trades and covered call trading are both effective trading methods; nevertheless, it is important to keep a look out for the upcoming fall.

Declining

Traders continue to hunt for fresh possibilities when the market is in a declining phase, which causes the stock to begin selling off. Shorting, covered calls, credit spreads, and covered puts are all fantastic possibilities that may be utilized as trading pattern tactics throughout the dropping portion of the market. If you can determine where a stock is in its lifecycle and what phase it is now in, you will have a far better chance of keeping the money you've worked so hard to gain and becoming a profitable trader.

Before Entering a trade

Focus on the following before entering a trade:

Volume

Two of the strategies that expert traders utilize are called volume over time profiling and watching the volume plotted against the price. The volume is the only leading signal that can be detected.

It is the method that professional traders use to understand whether an equity is accumulating prior to an up momentum move or if it is distributing prior to a down momentum move, respectively. Volume is used as a gauge by professional traders to determine the level of investor interest in the market. One may determine if there are more buyers or more sellers for a certain equity by examining the Volume distribution graph. Utilizing this knowledge enables one to more ef-fectively put their trading plans into action.

Volume at Price

The Volume by price is able to provide information that is signif-icantly more essential than that provided by normal volume indicators, which simply display quanti-ties at a certain moment. This information is the volume at a particular price. Paying close attention to the quantity of volume offered at a given price is something that should be done frequently. These are often solid support or resistance levels, and when a stock approaches these zones, one should be careful of the changes that are likely to follow.

The depth of the Volume by price is one factor that may be used to estimate the number of buyers and sellers currently in the market.

Volume at Time

After the price itself, the volume of data is the second most valuable piece of information.

A high volume suggests that there are a significant number of market participants actively involved in the

fluctuation of the price, particularly financial institutions, which are accountable for the vast bulk of the turnover experienced by the market.

In order for financial institutions to participate in trading, they need to have a vested interest in the price being maintained at a particular level and be prepared to take action to physically alter the price.

Price action

Price action trading is more than just trading candlestick patterns; rather, it encompasses everything reading historical and current price movements, understanding market structure, identifying key areas of value, and trading along the path of least resistance using candlestick patterns as trade triggers.

In essence, price action trading involves using historical and current price movements to understand the structure of the market — whether it is trending or ranging — and then identifying the important price levels and looking for trade setups (candlestick patterns) in the path of least resistance, which could mean following the trend or playing a ranging market accordingly.

Volatility

Volatility is a term that refers to the level of uncertainty or risk associated with the extent of movements in the value of an investment. A higher level of volatility indicates that the value of an investment might possibly be spread out over a wider range of values. The price of a security can move drastically within a short period of time in either direction as a result of these fluctuations. A lower level of volatility indicates that the value of an investment does not vary substantially and is more stable over time.

Bollinger Bands

One way to tell is a stock is volatile is to look at the Bollinger bands. If the bands are close together than the stock has low volatility and if the bands are far apart then the stock has high volatility.

Beta

Another measure is the beta (or beta coefficient) of a stock which is a measure of how volatile it is in relation to the market as a whole. In financial markets, beta is a measure of the total volatility of a security's returns as compared to the returns of a comparable market. For example, a company with a beta value of 1.1 has normally moved 110 percent for every 100 percent change in the benchmark index, depending on the current price level of the stock.

In contrast, a stock with a beta of .9 has normally moved 90 percent for every 100 percent change in the underlying index, according to the S&P 500.

Time Frames

There are many time frames in a chart as discussed previously. When examining a chart be sure to look at multiple time frames to validate your findings. Don't just look at the 1 minute, check the 5-minute, 10-minute, and even larger time frames to ensure your plan fits with the stock movement.

Catalysts

A stock catalyst is defined as anything that causes a significant shift in the price of a stock, whether it be good or unfavorable. An earnings report, a merger, the introduction of a new product, a press release, a stock split, a statement from the company's CEO, or the passage of legislation in Congress are all examples of stock catalysts. Monitoring the news and understanding important dates (earnings, product conferences or events) will help you make informed decisions as to the entry and exit of a trading plan.

Market Strength

If market is going down or up it could affect the stock. We often hear the trend is our friend. This is true in most cases. If the market is green and moving in an upward direction most equities will move in sync.

If the market is moving in a downward trend, then most equities will follow. We should always look at the overall market and the various sectors to understand the current status of the existing trend we are choosing to trade. If you are looking to invest in AMD, then we should look at the Technology ETF(XLK), and QQQ (tracks the Nasdaq 100 index which are the largest and most active companies trading on the Nasdaq Exchange and is formally known as QQQQ) to see the overall trend of the sector. The following is a list of the ETFs for the US Sectors:

Trading Setups

Having a trading plan ready to go for an upcoming trade is essential. Understand your entry point, your exit strategy (winning or losing), and your stop loss are all key to have in every trading strategy. when to take profit and when to take a stop loss. Only, after having all of these items in place, are you ready to begin trading. Let's get started!

U.S. Sector
ETF or ETN
Energy (XLE)
Real Estate (XLRE)
Technology (XLK)
Financial Services (XLF)
Consumer Staples (XLP)
Healthcare (XLV)
Utilities (XLU)
Basic Materials (XLB)
Consumer Discretionary (XLY)
Industrial (XLI)
Communication Services (XLC)

Putting it all together

In this book we have covered various trading strategies which we need to learn to put into practice. In order to do this, open a trade account and use paper trading for the first several months before making any trade with your own money. Practice and learn to look for the patterns discussed and create your trading plan and stick with it. As a recap some of the trading strategies we discussed are the following:

Moving averages

Follow the trends if a stock is above or below the 20-day, 100-day or 200-day moving average it is moving in a positive direction. Viewing several time frames to validate your findings is key. Buying stock or option calls during these upward trends is ideal for making a profit and puts for the downward trends.

RSI – Oversold and Overbought Crossover

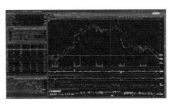

When a stock goes into over bought or oversold areas on a Stochastic RSI indicator, there is a favorable sign that a stock could move in the opposite direction. If a stock is oversold it is favorable the stock will begin an upward move. If a stock is overbought it could be on a momentum move that could last many days or even weeks, however it could also mean a favorable move in a downward direction.

Bollinger Bands

Two popular strategies

Trade the Bands: When the stock is at the top sell when it hits the bottom buy.

The Squeeze: When the bands shrink purchase in the direction of the trend.

Keltner Channels

Similar to the Bollinger Bands are two Popular strategies

Trade the Bands: When the stock is at the top sell when it hits the bottom buy.

The Squeeze: When the bands shrink purchase in the direction of the trend.

Squeeze

When a stock is in the accumulation phase, the Bollinger bands and the Keltner channel begin to shrink, as this occurs the bands and channels tighten to the point where they will pop in an upward or downward direction, normally in the direction of the trend.

Moving Average Convergence Divergence

MACD Cross over -If a stock is moving higher and the MACD indicator is showing the opposite position this could mean a reversal is not far behind. When the next cross over occurs a market correction could be in store.

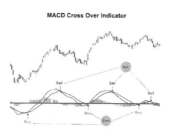

Watch them and as they develop, prepare your trading plan and your entry and exit strategies. When it reaches an entry point pull the trigger and then place a stop loss in place.

Trading Steps

Before making any trade, perform a trade verification:

Step 1 Look at the Overall Market - IS your trade going with the trend of the Market?

Step 2: Look at the Sector It the sector trending in the same direction of your trade?

Step 3: Where is the price in regard to the 50 and 200 day moving average, is it going with the trend?

Step 4: For Options add the in the call and put options cost together to understand the market expected move. 20-dollar stock 2-dollar call and 2 dollar put price movement (18 to 22 dollars)

Step 5: Understand the Risk to reward (IS it 1:1, 2:1,3:1,4:1) The better the odds the better the trade.

The divergence on the RSI graph is showing a possible reversal in the near future. Keeping an eye on other indicators to validate your findings will be worth its weight in gold.

It would be great to have indicators that provide you rapidly a snapshot of the equity that you are considering trading in order to facilitate the process of locating these kinds of trading setups. You should be able to scan for these kinds of settings so that you can quickly glance at a chart and decide whether or not this is an opportunity that is suitable for you. In addition, it would be helpful to have the capacity to do so.

Indicators and Scanning Opportunities

See the below scripts that can be used to make a custom scan filter in the TOS platform. We use Think or Swim because it is free, and it has all the tools one needs to invest wisely. The following scripts are used to find new opportunities and to validate our findings. For example, if a squeeze is occurring, we can check the Bollinger bands and the Keltner Channels to see if they are both contracted. This is a normal sign that volatility is low and that eventually something is going to give either to the upside or to the downside. Normally it will follow the trend. There is an indicator that can be used called TTM Squeeze to identify the squeeze. For more information about the possible indicators and scans please go to: https://tosindicators.com/scans

TTM Squeeze Indicator

The TTM Squeeze is a momentum and volatility indicator that was introduced by John Carter which is great visual representation of a squeeze. Identify these opportunities by using a scanner and create a watch list of these types of setups. Watch them and as they develop, prepare your trading plan and your entry and exit strategies. When it reaches an entry point pull the trigger and then place a stop loss to protect your investment.

Setting up a Scan

The following are instructions on how to setup the Squeeze, MACD Cross Over and the RSI Scans. Each of these can be used to scan for opportunities and the indicators can be used to validate your findings. In order to setup an indicator please go to Think or Swim and perform the following:

- Log into your account

- In the top right corner select studies

- Select add studies

- Then look through the list and find the study of your choice.

- The following studies / indicators we will be discussing and can be found in the list of studies are TTM_Squeeze, MACD Crossover and RSI

If you have difficulty follow-
ing our examples, please use the
following for the TTM Squeeze
setup in Think or Swim plat-
form (TOS) for a more thorough

guide: https://www.simplertrading.com/blog/trading-tips-strategies/ho
w-to-use-the-ttm-squeeze/

Setting up Scanners

In order to setup a scanner you need to login to TOS and navigate to Scan and select the Stock Hacker tab. On this tab you can set conditions for a new scan.

All of the scans we setup are used
to scan all stocks. Please use the
following examples to setup new
scanners on the Think or Swim
platform.

Follow the following instructions for each of these scanners.

- Select All Stocks

- Add scan filters by clicking on the Add filter button (located on the right side).

- The filters will be stacked in the groups with default para-meters

- Adjust your scan criteria by using the following to set each filter.

- Click Scan

- To save your query, click on the Show actions menu and select Save scan query

TTM Squeeze

Setting up a scanner for the
TTM_Squeeze in the Think or
Swim platform (TOS):

Standard Squeeze Scan

STOCK: Volume min 50K

STOCK: Last min $8

STUDY: TTM_Squeeze().SqueezeAlert == 0

STUDY: TTM_Squeeze()."SqueezeAlert" from 5 bars ago is equal
to 0

STUDY: TTM_Squeeze().SqueezeAlert == 0

Set it up for Hourly, Daily, Monthly,

MACD Crossover

Setting up the scanner for the
MCAD Cross Over setup scan:

- Market Cap is over 1 billion

- Volume over 450K

- Moving Average Scan at close is at least 0.0% Above the 34
  period Exponential moving average

- Moving Average Scan at close is at least 0.0% Above the 21
  period Exponential moving average

- Moving Average Scan at close is at least 0.0% Above the 8
  period Exponential moving average

- Moving Average Scan at close is at least 4.0% Above the 200
  period Exponential moving average

- Moving Average Scan at close is at least 1.0% Above the 55 period Exponential moving average

RSI

Setting up the scanner for the RSI Overbought and Oversold Scan:

- ALL Stocks

- Stock Price Min (last above) $6.00

- Volume over 50K (This is a scan that can be run right after the market opens, hence the low volume)

- RSI() "RSI" crosses below 30 or RSI() "RSI" crosses above 70

Once these scans are setup you can run each of them to find new opportunities. Each of the results can be saved and added to your watch list. Below are a couple of

links that will help you get this setup and running in no time at all:

https://tlc.thinkorswim.com/center/howToTos/thinkManual/Scan/Stock-Hacker

and

https://tlc.thinkorswim.com/center/howToTos/thinkManual/Getting-Started/Customizing-thinkorswim/Create-and-Customize-Watchlists.html

When first starting out as a trader the best thing you can do is learn and not lose your money. Open a paper trading account and pick one stock or ETF. We recommend the QQQ (tracks the NASDAQ) or

SPY (tracks the S&P 500) and watch them over a period of time to
see how they react to the overall market. Learn to notice the dips and
the rallies that occur within one ETF along with the zones, support
and resistance levels on multiple time frames. Look for a zone that the
ETF is moving around and find your entry and exit points. Check your
indicators to validate your findings. Once you have established these
areas of opportunity then plan your trade. When entering a trade, it is
essential you place a stop loss. A stop loss will help protect you from
losing your hard-earned money.

Chapter Eleven

Conclusion

N ow that you have been provided with the necessary knowledge for the market, it is time to put your knowledge into action. If you read this book, you will note that the issue of practicing comes up quite a bit. This is intentional. It is recommended that you practice with a demo account for three to six months before committing your actual money to the stock market before you begin trading.

While this may appear to be an excessive approach, it is necessary to assist you in becoming more familiar with the market. Furthermore, because you will require time to observe all of the possible moves in the market, there will be situations where you will not witness trend changes, breakouts, and reversals until several weeks or even months after they occur. As a result, if you rush into the market with your real money, you may end up with scorched fingers.

Another characteristic that you must possess in order to be a great trader is patience, as well as sound money management abilities. As we have seen in the numerous charts and examples provided in this book, there are circumstances in which the chart will provide misleading or unconfirmed signals, which may result in the loss of funds in the trading account. Additionally, your money management abilities should be activated both before and after you enter a deal. Every trade, regardless of whether it is lucrative or not, must have an exit objective.

Make a point of returning to this book as you practice each of the technical tools we have taught you. You should alter the time frame on your chart from time to time, even if you are an intraday trader, so that you can observe how the market looks from different time frames and perspectives.

It's now time to choose a platform and begin putting everything you've learned into practice. In the event that you enjoyed this book and learning about chart patterns, please take a moment to leave a five-star review on the site from which you purchased this edition. Hopefully, this will encourage more individuals to read and learn along with us and also help them become better stock traders in the long run.

Chapter Twelve

References

Standard Deviation Indicator. Fidelity Learning Center. https://www.fidelity.com/learning-center/trading-investing/technical-analysis/technical-indicator-guide/standard-deviation

Standard Deviation (Volatility). Stock Charts School. https://school.stockcharts.com/doku.php?id=technical_indicators:standard_deviation_volatility

Jeff, B (February 2020). Fundamental Analysis - Understanding the Standard Deviation of a Stock. Raging Bull. https://ragingbull.com/fundamental-analysis/standard-deviation-of-a-stock/

Simple Keltner Trading Strategy Explained. Forex Training Group. https://forextraininggroup.com/simple-keltner-channel-trading-strategies-explained/

Kshitiz, K. Technical Analysis - Bollinger Bands, and Keltner Channel Trading Strategy. https://mudrex.com/blog/bollinger-band-and-keltner-channel-trading-strategy/

Learn How to Calculate Keltner Channel before Your Next Trade. Commodity.

https://mudrex.com/blog/bollinger-band-and-keltner-channel-trading-strategy/

Keltner Channels. Stock Chart School.

https://school.stockcharts.com/doku.php?id=technical_indicators:keltner_channels

Cory M. (July 2021) Technical Analysis - Keltner Channel Definition. Investopedia.

https://www.investopedia.com/terms/k/keltnerchannel.asp

Moving Averages - Simple and Exponential Moving Averages. Stock Chart School.

https://school.stockcharts.com/doku.php?id=technical_indicators:moving_averages

Day Trading Encyclopedia. Investor Underground

https://www.investorsunderground.com/stock-charts/introduction/

James, C. (September 2021). Technical Analysis of Stocks and Trend Definition. Investopedia

https://www.investopedia.com/terms/t/technical-analysis-of-stocks-and-trends.asp

Jeff, D. (May 2017). 12 Types of Technical Indicators Used by Stock Traders. Visual Capitalist.

https://www.visualcapitalist.com/12-types-technical-indicators-stocks/

Leslie, K. (May 2021). An Overview of Bulls and Bear. Investopedia.

https://www.investopedia.com/insights/digging-deeper-bull-and-bear-markets/

Basic Candlesticks. Candlesticker.

https://www.candlesticker.com/BasicCandlesticks.aspx?lang=en

How to Read Candlestick Charts. Warrior Trading.

https://www.warriortrading.com/how-to-read-candlestick-charts
/

Japanese Candlesticks Basics. XGlobal Markets.

https://www.xglobalmarkets.com/learn_center/japanese-candlest
ick-basics/

Adam, M. (May 2021) How to Read Candlestick Charts. The Balance.

https://www.thebalance.com/how-to-read-a-candlestick-chart-10
31115

Barbara R. Basics of Candlestick Chart in Technical Analysis. Dummies.

https://www.dummies.com/personal-finance/investing/technical
-analysis/basics-of-candlestick-charts-in-technical-analysis/

11 Most Essential Stock Chart Patterns. CMC Markets.

https://www.cmcmarkets.com/en/trading-guides/stock-chart-pat
terns

Blain R. 5 Best Order Types for Stock Trading. Stock Trader.

https://www.stocktrader.com/order-types

Blain, R. (July 2021) How to Read Stock Charts (2021 Ultimate Guide).

https://www.stocktrader.com/how-to-read-stock-charts

Schwab Training Center. Schwab Training Center.

https://www.schwab.com/resource-center/insights/content/mast
ering-the-order-types-stop-limit-orders

16 Candlestick Pattern Every Trader Should Know. IG.

https://www.ig.com/en/trading-strategies/16-candlestick-patterns
-every-trader-should-know-180615

Marianna, G. (April 2021). Using Bullish Candlestick Patterns to Buy Stock.

https://www.investopedia.com/articles/active-trading/062315/us
ing-bullish-candlestick-patterns-buy-stocks.asp

Cory M. (April 2021). How to Use a Moving Average to Buy Stock.
Investopedia.

https://www.investopedia.com/articles/active-trading/052014/ho
w-use-moving-average-buy-stocks.asp

Moving Averages - Simple and Exponential. Chart School.

https://school.stockcharts.com/doku.php?id=technical_indicator
s:moving_averages

When To Use And How To Read The MACD Indicator.

https://commodity.com/technical-analysis/macd/

Made in United States
Orlando, FL
26 April 2023

32487291R00102